Neil Forsyth is an author, journalist and
Dundonian and friend to Bob Servant for
assisted Servant on two books, *Delete*
Emails and *Bob Servant – Hero of D*
series *The Bob Servant Emails*.

Forsyth is also the author of *Other People's Money*, the biography of
fraudster Elliot Castro, and the novel *Let Them Come Through*.

Praise for Bob Servant (*Delete This at Your Peril* and *Bob Servant – Hero of Dundee*)

'A former cheeseburger magnate and semi-retired window cleaner, Bob
is a delightfully deranged but likeable rogue. Drinking in and chasing
'skirt' around the bars of Broughty Ferry with ne'er-do-well mates such
as Frank the Plank, he is a late middle-aged working-class eccentric in
the vein of John Shuttleworth . . . a living, breathing creation of comic
genius . . . Today, Broughty Ferry. Tomorrow, the world?
Bookbag

'A very, very funny book. You will piss yourself and then quote sections
of this book repeatedly within your circle of friends'
Irvine Welsh

'Reminds me how good good comic writing can be . . . The surrealism is
perfect'
Scotland on Sunday

'This is one of the funniest books ever compiled . . . the work of a
comedy genius'
The Skinny

'Neil has captured something particular of the Dundonian, surreal sense
of humour. And I don't think we've ever had that before. We've had Billy
Connolly and Lex McLean's Glasgow stories and traditions, but now
we've got this Dundee creature who is just so funny . . . I was in hysterics'
Brian Cox

'Hilarious, full of sly, Scottish humour'
Martin Kelner, The Guardian

'He's a Henry Root for the digital age . . . a hilarious collection'
GT Magazine

'Hurrah for Bob Servant! Read it in private as it will make you laugh out loud'
The Book Magazine

'Brilliant entertainment. Funny, absurd, engaging comedy'
Felix Dexter

'Bob is a serious man, a thoughtful man, a complicated man, who knows that when holding a man's cock in the bathroom you look straight ahead'
Sharp Magazine

'There's stuff in here that Chic Murray would have been proud of'
Sanjeev Kohli

'Wildly unpredictable, roaringly funny'
Daily Express

'Some of the funniest emails you will ever read and some of the best comedy I have read in a while'
Lunch.com

'These are the writings of a clearly deranged mind'
Soteria

'*Delete This at Your Peril* will not win the Booker Prize'
The Kilkenny Advertiser

'★☆☆☆☆ – Didn't do it for me, a bit lazy . . . I just didn't connect to Bob as a person'
M. Thomas, Amazon.co.uk

Why Me?

Also by Neil Forsyth featuring Bob Servant

Bob Servant – Hero of Dundee

Delete This at Your Peril – The Bob Servant Emails

Fiction

Let Them Come Through

Non-fiction (with Elliot Castro)

Other People's Money. The Rise and Fall of Britain's Most Audacious Fraudster

Why Me?

The Very Important Emails of Bob Servant

Neil Forsyth

BIRLINN

First published in 2011 by
Birlinn Limited
West Newington House
10 Newington Road
Edinburgh
EH9 1QS

2

www.birlinn.co.uk

ISBN: 978 1 78027 009 8
eBook ISBN: 978 0 85790 093 7

Picture credits
pp. 4, 39, 42, 72 (left), 73 (left), 134 supplied by the author
pp. 15, 19, 82, 83, 114, 130, 131 by Mark Blackadder
All other artwork supplied by Getty Images

British Library Cataloguing-in-Publication Data
A catalogue record for this book is available
from the British Library

Typeset by Brinnoven, Livingston
Printed and bound by Clays Ltd, St Ives plc

For Rhiannon, my skirt, with love

Contents

Introduction by Neil Forsyth

Two bewildering decades have passed since I first met Bob Servant. Over that time I have encountered him as a window cleaner, a startlingly successful cheeseburger van operator and, in the last few years, an author of books which I have been given the task of editing. This is his third book and, as when I worked with him on the others, a part of me hopes it will be his last.

Bob's recent emergence as Scotland's least likely man of letters has caught most by surprise while apparently pleasing others. For them, a new addition to the Servant collection is perhaps greeted with a shade of excitement. For me it has meant the usual hardship. I know these are the first words you're encountering in a book bought for light diversion, and I apologise for the negativity, but I find it hard to offer an upbeat alternative.

My suffering began with Bob's standard approach to me in these matters, a phone call bristling with hubris and mild aggression. He had been 'back on the emails' and 'the results speak for themselves'. I was instructed to return with immediate effect to our shared hometown of Dundee – Scotland's sunniest city that sits in honest contemplation by the River Tay.

Reluctantly I boarded a train, to be met by Bob at Dundee's gleaming station. He had commandeered an aging Ford Sierra from a local pub landlord and took me on a tour of the city – sweeping up the Dundee Law hill to gaze down on the streets below, zipping between the glory-drenched football stadiums, crawling respectfully past the city centre's Desperate Dan statue and then finally down into the riverside suburb of Broughty Ferry, Bob's personal fiefdom.

It is in Broughty Ferry that Bob feels truly at home, and to see him marching through the streets is an astonishing sight. He liberally dispenses nods and winks to those he passes, whether they know him or not, and his hands are busy with shakes, pats and various tweaks which are greeted with delight by children and an often extreme discomfort by adults. The sight of Bob roughhousing with an uncooperative traffic warden, who was on the verge of tears throughout, remains disappointingly fresh in my mind.

Finally we retreated to Bob's favoured Stewpot's Bar where he told me of his plans for the book you currently hold. I asked, hesitantly, if a sequel of further emails was in any way a cash-in.

'World War Two was a sequel,' said Bob gravely. 'Was that a cash-in? Was beating the Nazis a cash-in?'

When Bob is in this kind of form, and I'm not sure I've ever seen him in another, there is little to be gained by debate. Instead I visited his ludicrous house the following morning and gathered the emails he had exchanged with spammers around the world.

For the third occasion I found myself in Dundee's central library for long weeks, trying to piece together a Bob Servant book. The emails themselves were as intriguing as ever, but as usual I was soon immersed in the library's *Dundee Courier* archive in my loyal attempt to stand up Bob's more unlikely claims. You will observe my woe through the book's editorial footnotes.

Two months later, drained by 12-hour days with Bob's inanity, I stood on his doorstep with the edited proof in my hands. As always I was seeking to leave Dundee after my tasks were done to avoid Bob's excitement as publication approached. I have heard various stories about Bob's behaviour in the days after last year's book release, when his titles sailed to the top of Dundee Waterstone's famously impregnable charts and Bob made an appearance on Grampian Television that still provokes local debate.

Bob led me to his living room where he'd been relaxing with an indeterminate alcoholic cocktail and an episode of the *You've Been Framed* television show which I noticed, with alarm, was not being transmitted but was playing from VHS video.

'This clip is top three,' said Bob sincerely while we watched a man sit on a plastic bin at a family barbecue before the bin's lid gave way, sucking the man within it while screaming family members ran to his aid. 'Not of all time,' added Bob helpfully, 'just of that series.'

I gave Bob the book's proof and mentioned the Acknowledgements section. He told me to come and find him the next day and that we would 'have a good time', a phrase which, when used by Bob, always means that I am going to have a bad time.[1]

After this burst of co-operation he grew distant once more, dividing his attention between myself and a compilation of people suffering mishaps in and around small rivers, streams and recreational lakes. Bob confided that he lacked appreciation for *You've Been Framed* clips involving people falling into water because they were 'as predictable as Christmas' and there was 'no real twist'.

I stood, shook Bob's hand and left him giggling quietly to himself, the mysterious cocktail close by and an endless stream of infantile entertainment flickering before him. In retrospect, I don't think I have ever seen him so happy.

Neil Forsyth
London
2011

---

1 See the Acknowledgements section, where I have a bad time.

A Big 'Hello' from Bob Servant

You know what? People think it's easy being me, but it's not. They see the big house and the extension and all my jumpers and so on and they think 'He's got it easier than Mandela'. But I don't. Because, like Mandela, my smile is just a frown in fancy dress and I'm under pressure. Terrible, terrible pressure.

When people see me in the street here in Dundee they all want a joke or a story. They want me to give them a wee slap or do something with my eyes that they think is just for them. It's knackering and after a while it just gets too much. As a result I've found myself staying in the house more and more these days. When I'm sitting here in my pyjamas I can have an honest drink or bite to eat without being pestered by the punters and the boo boys. I just want to hide from the world, like Greta Garbo or Terry Wogan.

That's what got me back on the computer. Talking to the Internet brigade is how I spend my days because you know where you are with this mob. They're cowboys, yes, I accept that but people forget that cowboys weren't all bad. Cowboys treated their horses like princesses and how many of us can honestly say that we've done the same? People who live in greenhouses shouldn't throw bricks.

That bit there about the horses was a metaphor really because, when it comes to the emails, I am like a jockey. I pick my rides and I get them to the end of the course but I don't always go the right way round the track. Sometimes I'll jump over the fence and trample on some of the punters but one way or another I'll be there at the winning post, with my head held high and my face covered with the punters' blood.

Come ride with me.

Bob Servant
Dundee
2011

Neil Forsyth (left) and Bob Servant, Broughty Ferry, 2011

An aged man is but a paltry thing,
A tattered coat upon a stick, unless
Soul clap its hand and sing

William Butler Yeats (1865–1939)

I have a great deal of company in the house, especially in the morning
when nobody calls.

                    Henry David Thoreau (1817–1862)

Life's like a box of spanners, David. You choose a spanner and you stand
there and say, 'Oh look at me with my spanner.' Hang on. Sorry, I think I
meant hammers, not spanners. Christ, what is it? Look, David, what I'm
saying is this: 'Put down your spanner and have a good time.'

                    Bob Godzilla Servant (1945–)

I

Why Me? 1

From: Rose
To: Bob Servant
Subject: Why Me?

Hello dear,
My name is Rose. I am 24 years old and am residing in the refugee camp
in Sudan as a result of the civil war in my country. Please listen to this
important information. My late father was the managing director of a
major Factory and he was the personal advicer to the former head of state
before the rebels attacked our house and killed my mother and my father
in cold blood. It was only me that is alive now and I managed to make my
way to this camp.

When my father was alive he deposited money in one of the leading
banks in Europe which he used my name as the next of kin. The amount
in question is $9.3 (Nine Million three Hundred Thousand US Dollars).
And i have contacted the bank so that i can have the money to start a
new life but they requested that i should have a foreign partner as my
representative due to my living status here. I know that you would be a
proper person for this. I know already that I trust you. I need only your
information.

Yours in love

Rose

From: Bob Servant
To: Rose
Subject: Why You Indeed, My Friend, Why You Indeed

Rose,
Thanks for writing. I hope you're having a lovely time at your summer camp
and aren't staying up too late with the other girls talking about boys!
Your email got me thinking. I recently published a book of email exchanges

with people much like yourselves where we had a bit of a mess about and so forth but no-one got hurt and, if you have the time, I wondered if you would be interested in taking part in a sequel?

Your Servant,

Bob Servant

From: Rose
To: Bob Servant
Subject: I rejoice to hear from you

Good Day Mr Bob
I rejoice from reading your mail. We can now have this money from the bank and have a new life together. You are a good man Bob and now please send the details below. It is so hard here in the refugee camp Bob the people have nothing.

(1)Your Full name:
(2)Your Phone number:
(3)Your Contact address:
(4)Your Age:
(5) Bank Name:
(6) Bank Address:
(7) Number of Account:
(8) International Account Routing Number:

Remain blessed

Rose

From: Bob Servant
To: Rose
Subject: Hello Again

Rose,
Great to hear from you again so quickly. I'm sorry you're not enjoying yourself at the camp but at least you seem to have a computer and rapid Internet access.

Thanks for the opportunity to give you all my information. I try regularly to give women my information and usually they pretend they're not interested, but here's you actually asking for it. Having said that I'm going to say 'thanks but no thanks' to the banking stuff because I am worried that if I became a multi-millionaire I'd alienate my hardcore fans like what happened with Bruce Springsteen and Aneka Rice.

However, I have now firmly decided to crack on with this new book and would love you to be involved.

Bob

From: Rose
To: Bob Servant
Subject: Fill in the FORM

Bob,
Yes I have a computer but it is very old and I hide it from the others at the camp so it is not stolen. Bob send your information below. It is due now. I do not know what you mean about this book.

(1)Your Full name:
(2)Your Phone number:
(3)Your Contact address:
(4)Your Age:
(5) Bank Name:
(6) Bank Address:
(7) Number of Account:
(8) International Account Routing Number:

Remain blessed

Rose

From: Bob Servant
To: Rose
Subject: RE: Fill in the FORM

Rose,
No problem, let me make it even clearer. I am writing a book that is a collection of my exchanges with Internet cowboys like your good self. What happens is I have a wee chat with you and then we shake hands and go our separate ways. You wouldn't get any money from me but you'd see your name in print and it would be a funny story to tell your pals.

Let me know if you are available.

Thanks,

Bob

PS I attach a photo of the Dundee Waterstone's bestseller chart from Christmas. As you'll see I'm at number 1 AND number 4. That's the kind of form you used to get from the Beatles for fuck's sake Rose.

From: Rose
To: Bob Servant
Subject: NO

OF COURSE I WILL NOT BE PART OF THAT. WHY WOULD I DO
THIS? YOU THINK I HAVE TIME FOR THAT?

From: Bob Servant
To: Rose
Subject: That's Your Decision And I Will Respect It 100%

Fair enough. I'll try some others.

NO REPLY

2

Bob the Oilman

From: Alan Thompson
To: Bob Servant
Subject: National Oil and Investment

Welcome to National Oil and Investment. I have come to you because I believe you are a man to be trusted and who will understand business. Tell no-one about this opportunity.

I am American man currently working here in Togo to drill and sell the best OIL. Due to over production at our plant in Togo we are in a lucky position to send you thousands of OIL free of charge. Because this is a secret deal with no tax to pay you will pay only the shipment fee and the goods will be yours to distribute in your own country. You can sell one barrel of OIL for $175. Shipment is $50,000 for 50,000 barrels of oil so you can see the profit to be made.

Looking forward to hearing from you soonest,

Mr Alan Thompson
Director
National Oil And Investment
Royal Plaza
Togo

From: Bob Servant
To: Alan Thompson
Subject: Oil Me Up

Alan,
The warmest greetings imaginable from Broughty Ferry, Dundee. Your email is one of the most exciting business opportunities that I have received by email from Western Africa this morning, and I can't offer much higher praise than that.

I would love to be in the oil game Alan. Being from Dundee we have to deal with the Aberdeen oil mob up the road and it's hard work. I don't mind people being rich, God knows I'm not short of a penny, but I like it when they wear their wealth with quiet dignity like Her Majesty the Queen and Jimmy Savile. The Aberdeen mob are very much Novo Reach. They rub their oil money in your face (not in a saucy way) with their nice jumpers, matching shoes and high-end Ford Sierras.

This wee 'back door' into the oil business could be a chance not just for me, but for Dundee as a city to bounce back. It's certainly exciting. I used to love that big American TV show about the family with all the oil money. The main guy wore a special hat and used to make long, inspirational speeches. Did you see it? I think it was called The Cosby Show.

Your Servant,

Bob Servant

From: Alan Thompson
To: Bob Servant
Subject: National Oil and Investment

Dear Bob Servant,
CONGRATULATIONS! You have been accepted as a new customer for us. Let us start the administration straight away so you can have your OIL soon enough. I do not know this television show but I can tell you Bob that with the money you will make you will feel like you are on the television. Now fill this form and send back for immediate processing.

FULL NAME:
CONTACT ADRESS:
PHONE NUMBER:
SEX:
AGE:
OCCUPATION:
COUNTRY:
STATE:
MATIRIAL:

Looking forward to hear from you soon

Mr Alan Thompson

Director
National Oil and Investment
Royal Plaza
Togo

From: Bob Servant
To: Alan Thompson
Subject: TV

Alan,

As much as I like you Alan, I certainly don't want to feel like I'm on television after an awful experience I had last year. A so-called friend (Chappy Williams, the snake) convinced me that I was being interviewed for Blind Date but it turned out that I was actually on some Grampian TV nonsense.[2]

That aside, does this mean I have the job? Or should I say your job?

Bob

From: Alan Thompson
To: Bob Servant
Subject: The Job Is Yours

Yes Bob you have the job! so please send the form.

Mr Alan Thompson

Director
National Oil and Investment
Royal Plaza
Togo

From: Bob Servant
To: Alan Thompson
Subject: Your Forthcoming Retirement

Alan,

I will have a good look at the form later today. It's great to be on board and cheers for appointing me to your job. I would like to thank you for all your work and wish you the best of luck for the future. As I will tell the lads at your retirement dinner, if I can be half the man you were, then I'll be happy! PS recognise these little guys?

---

2 See Grampian TV's *Local Spotlight* programme on 5 October 2010 where Bob appears in a confusing three-minute segment. Bob clearly believes he is filming a taped audition for a television dating show. He continually speaks directly to the camera, against standard convention, to confide various physical attributes and capabilities that often veer to the lewd. The interview ends with Bob topless, struggling to lift a park bench and urging viewers to 'call the number at the bottom of the screen' despite the fact that no such graphic is being displayed.

All the best,

Mr Bob Servant
Director
National Oil and Investment
Royal Plaza
Togo

From: Alan Thompson
To: Bob Servant
Subject: National Oil and Investment

Bob,

That is my job. You do not have a title as you are only a customer. Please fill in the form. What is this picture?
Mr Alan Thompson

Director
National Oil and Investment
Royal Plaza
Togo

From: Bob Servant
To: Alan Thompson
Subject: Eh?

Alan,
I don't quite follow what you're saying about the job title, as the situation seems pretty clear at my end. Anyway, we've got more important things to discuss which is – what stories can I tell at your retirement dinner? Are you bringing the missus or can I be a bit risqué? A little birdie told me about the conference in Tenerife where a certain someone let his hair down quite

spectacularly? There are whispers about you, a trolley dolly from Togo Airlines, a bath full of champers and a couple of dozen garden gnomes?

Kind Regards,

Mr Bob Servant
Director
National Oil and Investment
Royal Plaza
Togo

From: Alan Thompson
To: Bob Servant
Subject: National Oil and Investment

Bob,
You are not right in calling yourself this. It is my job, please stop. You are a customer. I am not going to retire why would I retire when I am young and there is so much money to be made? I have not been to Tenerife and don't know what this picture is about.

Send the form.

Mr Alan Thompson
Director
National Oil and Investment
Royal Plaza
Togo

From: Bob Servant
To: Alan Thompson
Subject: Make Your Mind Up

Alan,
Sorry you've completely lost me. One minute you're retiring and the next

minute you're not. One minute you're boasting to anyone who'll listen about a night with a trolly dolly and the next you've never been to Tenerife? What's going on? Are you OK? I'm worried about you.

Kind Regards,

Mr Bob Servant
Director
National Oil and Investment
Royal Plaza
Togo

From: Alan Thompson
To: Bob Servant
Subject: National Oil and Investment

Bob,
I want to get on with the OIL and send it to your country for you to make a lot of money but do you see that you are calling yourself my job? I am the DIRECTOR you are the CUSTOMER. Do you understand? Do you not know business? I am NOT for retiring now. I have NOT been to Tenerife with anybody. STOP sending these pictures.

Mr Alan Thompson
Director
National Oil and Investment
Royal Plaza
Togo

From: Bob Servant
To: Alan Thompson
Subject: Take It Easy

Alan,

Fine, you're not retiring and you want to keep the Tenerife stuff under wraps, I get it. But hold tight Alan, to accuse me of not knowing business is laughable. Where shall I begin? With the fact that in the late 1970s I had the longest windowcleaning round in Western Europe,[3] or the fact that in the late 1980s I had fourteen cheeseburger vans going like a train 24 hours a day?[4] Or shall we talk about me being Broughty Ferry Businessman of The Year twenty-three years running?[5]

You choose Alan. Just you choose. OK?

Kind Regards,

Mr Bob Servant
Alan Thompson's Best Pal and Hero
National Oil and Investment
Royal Plaza
Togo

From: Alan Thompson
To: Bob Servant
Subject: OK Fine Bob

Bob,

OK, let us just forget the job title situation as this does not matter. Yes we are now pals for sure and I did not mean to say you are not a businessman. You must be a famous businessman in your country if you have done all this. What matters Bob is your order being processed properly by us and you can get your OIL and make this big money. Please fill in the form and send back for immediate processing.

---

3 See *The Dundee Courier,* 16 February 1978: *'The Pitter Patter of Lots of Ladders'* ('Local man's windowcleaning round smashes 100-home barrier . . . "People said that was a glass ceiling," said Servant, "but I wash glass ceilings, that's the difference."')
4 See *The Dundee Courier,* various articles 1989–1991, such as 4 June 1990: *'Servant Wins Again'* ('Broughty Ferry cheeseburger magnate Bob Servant last night celebrated the unveiling of his fourteenth van and launched a defiant tirade against other van owners involved in what many have dubbed "The Cheeseburger Wars" . . . "Why are people calling it the Cheeseburger Wars?" asked Servant, "if anything it's a massacre. This is our Dunkirk, and I'm Rommel."')
5 See *The Dundee Courier,* 23 March, 1998. *'Dundee City Council Scraps Annual Award* ('endemic corruption' . . . 'terrified judges' . . . 'silent phone calls'.)

FULL NAME:
CONTACT ADRESS:
PHONE NUMBER:
SEX:
AGE:
OCCUPATION:
COUNTRY:
STATE:
MATIRIAL:

From: Bob Servant
To: Alan Thompson
Subject: My Garage Awaits

Alan,

I accept your apology and I'm glad we're back on track. I have started
sorting things out this end. Dundee is right on the River Tay so it shouldn't
be a problem reversing in your oil tanker. Once it's arrived then it will be
a case of getting the oil off and over to my house. I have a double garage
with a much admired 'cantilever roof' so 50,000 barrels of oil should fit no
bother at all.

Can you please give me the name of the ship and also the name of the
captain? I will fill in the form shortly, I'm just waiting for the right pencil to
make itself known.

Thanks,

Bob

From: Alan Thompson
To: Bob Servant
Subject: Use Any Pencil

Dear Mr Bob

That is fine and we will deliver 50,000 barrels free of charge, you will
simply pay the shipment. I will locate the name of the captain and his
ship shortly Bob. Use any pencil or pen you have to hand it does not
matter or best type it direct on the computer.

Mr Alan Thompson
Director NPC

From: Bob Servant
To: Alan Thompson
Subject: Here You Go

Alan,
No problem, info below, please send over the names of the ship and the captain.

Cheers Al,

Bob

FULL NAME: Bob Godzilla Servant
CONTACT ADRESS: Harbour View Road
PHONE NUMBER: No phone after I accidentally spent over £3,000 calling a phoneline that I believed was about wildlife[6]
SEX: Totally Male
AGE: 64
OCCUPATION: Businessman/Man About Town/A Good Guy To Have Around The Place
COUNTRY: UK/Scotland/Dundee/Broughty Ferry
STATE: Excited
MATIRIAL: Eh?

From: Alan Thompson
To: Bob Servant
Subject: National Oil and Investment

Bob,
Thank you for your response. It is not all there but it is enough for now. OK, this is the captain's name and ship name

Captain Newman
Ship name: Edmund

You want 50,000 barrels of oil. Shipment is therefore $50,000. Payment should be sent immediately through Western Union.

BANK NAME: ECO BANK LOME TOGO
ADDRESS: ██████████████████████
A/C NAME. ██████████████

---

6 See *The Dundee Courier*, 16 April 2010. *'Local Man Outraged by Porn Swindle'* ('"Maybe I'm old fashioned," said Servant, "but to me a phone line calling itself Cougar Hunters should be about safaris" . . . Servant said he was "absolutely disgusted" by what he heard during a series of calls of up to an hour, made over a two-week period.')

A/C NUMBER: ███████████
SWIFT CODE: ███████████
DESTINATION: LOME TOGO WEST AFRICA

As soon as you transfer the fee, send me the transfer slip for confirmation and immediate processing. Looking forward to hearing from you,

Mr Alan Thompson

Director

From: Bob Servant
To: Alan Thompson
Subject: The Dundee Courier

Alan,
Thanks for the account info and it's good of your friend to let you use his bank account for such a hefty wedge, you must trust that boy like there's no tomorrow.

   Anyway, exciting news. A little birdie (not the same one I mentioned before) tipped off the Dundee Courier (our local rag) and they've done a bit of a splash on our link-up this morning, the article is attached below. Also can I just check what we are talking in terms of crew numbers? I will tell you right now that I will not have the crew staying in my gaff (known around Dundee as 'Bob's Palace'[7]). It's not that kind of place. They can either stay at my neighbour Frank's house or if there's a few of them then I will sort something else out. But Captain Newman (I like him already!) will have his pick of the bedrooms at Bob's Palace, that's a promise. And if I break that promise, Alan, then you can break my arm.

With a fucking sledgehammer.

Thanks,

Bob

---

7 I have never heard anyone ever refer to Bob's house as 'Bob's Palace' apart from Bob, despite his repeated attempts to have others do so. He once sent himself a letter addressed to Bob's Palace which resulted in a two-hour, highly-charged stand-off with his postman which left both men emotionally scarred.

The Dundee Courier 25 January 2011

Dundee in Shock Oil News

Dundee celebrated today after a local businessman pledged to create an oil industry to rival neighbouring Aberdeen and bring untold riches to the city. Broughty Ferry entrepreneur Bob Servant, well known from the city's so-called Cheeseburger Wars, has struck a deal with African giants National Oil to 'flood' the city with cheap oil.

'This is the moment that Dundee has been waiting for,' said Servant today. 'Aberdeen has been a thorn in our side for too long and it's time for Dundee to grab a slice of the pie while it's still hot. I am doing this for the city and it's all gravy from here.'

Servant claims National Oil will begin sending vast quantities of oil in the next few weeks, delivering 50,000 barrels at a time in their famed supertanker, the SS *Edmund*, crewed by 200 men and captained by a man Servant describes as the 'world famous' Captain Newman. 'Captain Newman and his men are the best in the business,' says Servant. 'They could sail here blindfolded and, knowing Captain Newman as I do, he probably will.'

Servant says he will import enough oil for Dundee's own use as well as a surplus amount to sell to other Scottish cities. 'Because we're getting the stuff for peanuts, we can undercut Aberdeen to our heart's content,' said Servant. 'Edinburgh will be like a rat up a drainpipe, and I think we'll all enjoy seeing Glasgow come to us cap in hand. I'm in two minds on Perth, as I'm sure we all are.'

A spokesman for Dundee City Council hailed Servant as 'a visionary' while Tayside Police welcomed the news. 'Although usually the illicit importation and sale of oil would be a concern from the lawmaking point of view,' said a spokesman, 'in this case we'll be turning blind eyes all over the shop.'

'Some people are suggesting that I'm a hero,' Servant told *The Courier* last night. 'That's their decision. What I will say is this. I remember Liz Lynch being called a hero. And she came second. That's all I'm going to say. Hopefully you see what I'm saying. Liz Lynch came second. If you read between the lines you will see what I'm saying. She came second, but did I? That's what I am saying. Between the lines.'

8

---

8 Lynch, Liz (1964–). Popular Dundonian silver medal winner at the 1988 Olympic Games in South Korea. See *The Dundee Courier*, 20 July 1988. *'Lynch on Top of The World'*. ('Dundee's Liz Lynch wowed the world yesterday in the Olympic Games 10,000m event . . . Lynch dominated the race from start to finish and the crowd gave a standing ovation to the invincible Dundonian . . . In a light-hearted touch to the day's events, Lynch technically came in second as nervous Russian runner Olga Bondarenko was so intimidated by Lynch that she ran away from the brave Scot and, in doing so, inadvertently won the race.')

From: Alan Thompson
To: Bob Servant
Subject: National Oil and Investment

Dear bob
am glad to hear the news of DUNDEE In Shock Oil. we are very proud
of you and we feel that the people will see you as a hero for sure. the
director board of administrations has agree to shipped the oil for you as
soon as poseble without any delay. we went to the bank to see if you have
make the payment but not yet done. why? Bob kindly go to your BANK
and make the payment today for immediate processing.

You are correct. The Ship will be about 200 crew members,

regard

Mr Alan Thompson
MD

From: Bob Servant
To: Alan Thompson
Subject: Dundee's Going Mad for Captain Newman

Alan,
A lot of excitement here about Captain Newman. He's really got people
talking. Men want to be him and women want to see him. Can I ask please,
what are his main hobbies? And will he be happy talking about being a
Captain and what other areas of conversation do you think he would want
to talk about? The reason I ask is that I know from bitter experience how
difficult captains can be.

In 1983 I bumped into Dundee United's league winning captain Paul
Hegarty in Safeways. He was standing next to the tinned fish aisle and
quick as a flash I said,

'Afternoon skipper, buying some kippers?'

It was a decent joke, not the best I've ever told (not even the best I've
ever told in the tinned fish aisle) but the way he looked at me Alan, my
God. It was a look that could have frozen the sun.

What I'm saying is this – Captains are unpredictable and sometimes
they don't like the same jokes as normal people. So I need to tread
carefully with Captain Newman and would like you to give me as much
extra info as you can.

Finally, please send me the names of the 200 crew members which I
presume you'll have close to hand in a file. It's so I can book their hostel
rooms. Nicknames are fine.

Bob

From: Alan Thompson
To: Bob Servant
Subject: National Oil and Investment

Dear bob,
Well Captain Newman likes all kinds of jokes and he likes everything
such as smoke and drink. I have spoken to him and he says this is a great
honour to stay with you at Bob's Palace.

Here are your crew names for the hotel.

AARON, ABA, ABAY, ABBA, ABBOTT, ABBY, ABCDE,
ABDIEL, ABDUKRAHMAN, ABDULKAREEM ABDULLAH,
ABDULRAHMAN, ABE, ABEDNEGO, ABEEKU, ABEL, ABELARD,
ABHAY, ABIE, ABIYRAM, ABNER, ABRAHAM, ABRAM,
ABSOLOM, ABU, ACE, ACHAVA, ACHILLES, ACOOSE, ACOTAS,
ACTON, ADAHY, ADAIR, ADAM, ADAN, ADARSH, ADDAE,
ADDISON, ADE, ADEBEN ADELIO, ADEM, ADEN, ADIEL, ADISH[9]

Now Bob it is time to send the payment

Alan

From: Bob Servant
To: Alan Thompson
Subject: The Names

Alan,
Thanks so much for those 200 names. At first I thought I could see some
sort of pattern with them but maybe I'm imagining it. You also left a link at
the bottom of your email to a website called 'Baby Names' so I presume
you and Mrs Thompson are expecting a little one. Congratulations, I hope
he or she grows up to respect you as much as I do.

For 200 people I think it would be best to stick them in the Sleep Tight
and Don't Fight Hostel in Lochee.[10] I will get the rooms booked up now. I
would estimate that the booking will also cost around $50,000 so shall we
just call it level on the money?

Finally, a few last questions on Captain Newman.

You said he likes to drink, what is his favourite drink?

He's obviously not shy of a party, is he a big fan of women (in Dundee we
call them skirt, which they like a lot)?

---

9 I have edited out the rest of these 200 names, which continue in a predictable
vein.
10 See *www.tripadvisor.com* Review entitled *'To Hell And Back'* ('anarchy' . . .
'keen sense of danger' . . . 'kung-fu kick . . . from the receptionist')

Does he sing any songs at parties?

How long has he been at sea?

He sounds like a mad dog, is he a mad dog?

Thanks,

Bob

From: Alan Thompson
To: Bob Servant
Subject: National Oil and Investment

Bob,
Answers below but that is it now, you must send the payment for the OIL
shipment. We will pay for the hostel ourselves because that is the way
we do business here. Captain Newman and I are both waiting. Come on
Bob, send this payment and you will make more money than you will
understand.

You said he likes to drink, what is his favourite drink? . . . RUM

He's obviously not shy of a party, is he a big fan of women (in Dundee we
call them skirt, which they like a lot)? . . . YES IF GOOD

Does he sing any songs at parties? . . . NO

How long has he been at sea? . . . 15 YEARS

He sounds like a mad dog, is he a mad dog? . . . OK YES.

From: Bob Servant
To: Alan Thompson
Subject: Game Over

Alan,
Big, big problems my end. I have been updating the folk here in Dundee
about Captain Newman and it's gone down like a lead balloon. The irony
is that the more that I hear about Captain Newman the more I like and
respect him, but for others it seems it's quite the opposite.

It's bad news all round I'm afraid. I tried a bit of 'firefighting' but
unfortunately The Courier got hold of the story and that's our goose
cooked.

The article's attached, there's no way back from this unfortunately.
When the folk round here turn on you, it's time to walk away, but when the
Dundee Skirt Protection League get on your tail, then it's time to run for the
hills.

All the best for the future, and please pass on my regards to Captain Newman and the crew. I can't believe I will never meet them in the flesh. Knowing that I will never see the SS Edmund sail down the Tay makes me feel like Colin Montgomerie has torn out my heart and stuck it in his deep freeze.

Your Servant,

Bob Servant

The Dundee Courier   30 January 2011

Dundee Rejects 'Mad Dog' Captain

Dundee closed ranks today against the proposed arrival in the city of an oil tanker captained by a man described by his own company representative as a 'mad dog'.

Captain Newman, of the SS *Edmund*, was supposed to be delivering the oil that would kick-start an oil industry in Dundee to rival that of Aberdeen. The news of the ship's impending arrival provoked local celebrations earlier this week but, as news emerged yesterday of Captain Newman's true character, Dundee awoke this morning with a sour taste in its mouth.

It was National Oil's Scottish representative Bob Servant whose comments at a media briefing this morning provoked panic.

'He's a mad dog,' shrugged Servant. 'That's what they call him. Look, the guy has been at sea for fifteen years and he's seen the lot – pirates, tidal waves, Fife. Who wouldn't lose their mind? But, yes, he's a loose cannon. I can't deny that. We deal in honesty at National Oil.'

'First and foremost he loves skirt,' continued Servant. 'He's skirt mad and he always has been. When I say "Lock up your daughters when Captain Newman is about" I really do mean "Lock up your daughters when Captain Newman is about" because otherwise absolutely anything can happen.'

'He also loves a drink,' added Servant, 'especially rum which he will do almost anything to get his hands on. And he smokes like a chimney, so good luck to anyone trying to enforce the smoking ban when the skipper's about! He'd rip their head off and throw away the key.'

Servant's words were greeted with dismay and fear by the authorities. A spokesman for Dundee City Council said 'National Oil are no longer welcome in the city,' while Tayside Police released a statement that Newman would be 'arrested on the spot' if he arrives in Dundee. A spokeswoman for the Dundee Skirt Protection League said they would be protesting outside Servant's humble Broughty Ferry home this weekend if the deal wasn't cancelled.

From: Alan Thompson
To: Bob Servant
Subject: Ignore what they are saying

Bob,
Forget all these troubles and SEND THE PAYMENT.
STRAIGHT AWAY

Alan

3

The Football and Timmy Servant

From: Dominic Jones
To: Bob Servant
Subject: If You Are Interested

Dear Friend

Dominic Jones is my name. I was an official in the last FIFA World Cup 2010 and was one of the people that in charge of the dressing room. I therefore have the opportunity to meet some of the world best players and now have 1 football and 1 Jersey with signatures of some of the best players that i met. Players like Cristiano Ronaldo, Messi, Wayne Rooney, Torres, Kaka, Didier Drogba, Paul Scholes and Carlos Tévez.

I am keeping the jersey for my son (Jerry) but am giving out the ball in the photo as a Christmas gift. I am not collecting money for the signatures cause I got it free of charge from them, only the ball money and delivery charges which is £187.746 GBP. Send me your Name and Address, if you are interested.

Mr Dominic Jones

From: Bob Servant
To: Dominic Jones
Subject: Postage

Dominic,
Thanks for getting in touch. Let's round that up to £188 shall we? Easier on the eye. I have to say Dominic that, while I wouldn't want to question your maths, that seems a pretty penny just for postage. Where do you live, the Milky Way?

It's a funny time to buy a Christmas gift, in the middle of March, but I have to say I'm interested.

Your Servant,

Bob Servant

From: Dominic Jones
To: Bob Servant
Subject: RE: Postage

I live here in Hong Kong so this is a fair price.

From: Bob Servant
To: Dominic Jones
Subject: Fair enough

Dominic,
OK that makes sense and it's wonderful to hear from someone in Hong Kong. The last person I know from Dundee who had pals in Hong Kong was Ralphie Milne.[11]

My God, what a time you must have had at the World Cup. Can you give me any good 'tales from the boot room'? Also, please say hello to your son Jerry, I think I bumped into him the other day on Broughty Ferry beach. He was wearing women's clothing and was extremely drunk. He

---

11 Milne, Ralph (1961–). Popular Dundonian footballer who played for various clubs including Manchester United. Late in his career Milne played for a year in Hong Kong after a trial that involved him dribbling round an Asian football agent in London's Green Park. This, believe it or not, is true.

said something about Italy? How he wanted to go to Italy to 'see all the men in their nice shoes'?

Bob

From: Dominic Jones
To: Bob Servant
Subject: Not The Right Jerry

Dear Bob,
First that would not be my son as he is only six years old now and lives here with me in Hong Kong. So that will be a different Jerry I am sorry. Yes I have many stories from my time at the World Cup but you must respect that this was my job and I cannot tell them to the public. Now Bob do you want the ball?

Dominic Jones

From: Bob Servant
To: Dominic Jones
Subject: Omerta

Dominic,
I can appreciate that there's probably a bit of an Omerta situation and a 'what happens in the dressing room, etc' mentality but if you could just give me a snippet that would help convince me this was all by the book? I hate to doubt you but I read a wee thing in the People's Friend magazine the other day about how the Internet's full of cowboys. I'm always having wee chats on the Internet with people I don't really know so, as you can imagine, reading that article made me feel like Pat Butcher was using my heart as a xylophone.

Bob

From: Dominic Jones
To: Bob Servant
Subject: OK I can tell you this

Well let me just say that the top players are very serious in the changing room Bob. They do not spend that period having a wild time or being involved with jokes because why would they? This is the most important time they have Bob. I will tell you that many of them pray both to God and their own family and have a massage. There now I think that shows you who I am.

I have a lot of interest Bob in this ball and my other merchandise so you must be quick.

Dominic Jones

From: Bob Servant
To: Dominic Jones
Subject: We're 'Leg Men' Round This House

Dominic,
You're right, I shouldn't have pushed you. You're one of the most respected World Cup Dressing Room Supervisors on the circuit and I apologise for suggesting you risk your job by giving me mindless gossip to impress the boo boys down at Stewpot's Bar.

I would absolutely love to buy this ball for my own son (Timmy). He has been getting into a lot of trouble at school which is causing considerable problems between me and my wife.[12] I say that Timmy's problems at school are because of the pressure she puts on him but she says it's because I encourage him to stay up all night with me watching American sports on Channel 5 and talking about skirt. That's insane because for a start he doesn't need any encouragement. We both love baseball and, when it comes to the skirt, we're both leg men so the conversation takes care of itself.

Anyway, your football could be the treat Timmy needs to buck up his ideas. Stick me down for it please.

Bob

From: Dominic Jones
To: Bob Servant
Subject: Payment Details

Dear Bob,
Thanks for getting back to me and please promise me you will treasure the ball it means a lot to me, I want you to go to any Western Union money transfer or money gram outlet close to you and make the payment of £188 as agreed. I promise, as soon as the payment is confirmed, the

---

12 The suggestion that Bob is or ever has been married is laughable. For reference read 'The Great Skirt Hunt' in *Bob Servant: Hero of Dundee* or save yourself £6.99 and simply observe the chapter title. The further erroneous suggestion that Bob has a child is the stuff of nightmares.

ball will be delivered to you in the next two days. Here is the information to use

Receivers Name: Mr Dominic Jones
Address: Hong Kong
Text Question: Who do you love most?
Text Answer: Jesus
Amount Paid: £188 GBP

Thanks

Dominic Jones

From: Bob Servant
To: Dominic Jones
Subject: My Pal The Ref

Dominic,
Thanks for turning down all the other people to reserve me the football. Timmy will be so happy. I can only imagine his little face when I surprise him at the breakfast table by whipping a signed football out from within the folds of my dressing gown.

I must admit that I let slip down at Stewpot's Bar that I am now pals with one of the world's most successful referees. My pal Frank had a question for you, Dominic. If someone took a shot at goal, and it was going in, and then Mussolini wasn't dead and he ran out the crowd and headed it clear, what's the situation? By the book the goal presumably shouldn't stand, but when it's Mussolini clearing it off the line then it would surely be very, very hard to justify chalking it off. Thoughts?

I have all the respect in the world for you, Dominic. And for Jerry, who is one of the bravest little boys going. I know he is sick but he is a fighter and that gives him an outside chance of making it.

Bob

From: Dominic Jones
To: Bob Servant
Subject: My answer to this

Hello Bob
My son Jerry is not sick who told you that? Yes the ball will be a perfect present for your son Timmy. I want someone who will value this ball and I now trust that this is your son Timmy. Please Bob, I was not a referee so it is not possible for me to deal with this Mussolini situation. My own feeling would be that it would be a goal still but that is only my feeling.

Remember I was not a referee I was appointed to work with them and to look after the dressing room and keep everything safe OK?

Thanks

Dominic Jones

From: Bob Servant
To: Dominic Jones
Subject: Quick Work

Dominic,
Well you didn't keep things that safe if you nicked a ball and a jersey did you?! Don't worry, I'm just jerking your chain, I can't blame you for grabbing some freebies. I agree with your reading of the Mussolini situation and with regards the ball both Timmy and I will value it very highly.

    I'm close to paying for it but I do have a slight issue. Surprise, surprise, my wife's being a right pain in the arse. She's bleating that footballers are a bad influence on Timmy because they are always spitting and talking about themselves in the 'third person' and she would rather that we buy him a football signed by doctors and lawyers. Dominic, you actually met these guys 'mano-oh-oh-mano'. What were they like? A decent mob?

PS Sorry about any misunderstanding over Jerry's health. My neighbour Frank thought he saw him on Casualty.

Bob

From: Dominic Jones
To: Bob Servant
Subject: They were all OK

Dear Bob
I hear all you say and am sorry for what you are passing through. Women are always the same everywhere, the only thing in life is endurance. Football players are like us they are human with body and flesh the only thing different is they are celebrities through profession. In every occupation you have good and bad people so I took my time to select the ones I met. I interacted with every single one and they are all good and friendly people. I understand what your wife says but please tell her they have good conscience and attitude. Please advice today if you can pay for the ball as I am shortly travelling to Canada on business issue to sell my merchandise.

Dominic Jones

From: Bob Servant
To: Dominic Jones
Subject: That Should Shut Her Up

Dominic,

Thanks so much. I have passed all this onto my wife and even she had to stop her whining and admit that the players sound like not bad lads. I did have one more question on that front, Dominic, I noticed that Paul Scholes was in the dressing room and signed the ball and jersey. It's just that he chucked playing for England a few years back[13] so I was just wondering what he was doing there? Had he lost his dog?

Yours,

Bob

PS The Canada thing was a bit of a 'namedrop' was it not? Me and Frank are thinking of heading to Pitlochry at the weekend to look for skirt but you won't hear us banging on about it!

From: Dominic Jones
To: Bob Servant
Subject: Back From Canada

Dear Bob

Thank you I am now back from Canada and I am pleased to say that I did many business while there and there was a lot of interest in my merchandise. The people there wanted this ball but I said of course that it was for you only. So Bob it is fair that you should pay for it now.

Paul Scholes was in the FIFA dressing room because he is friends with these players so of course he is allowed to visit them.

Dominic Jones

From: Bob Servant
To: Dominic Jones
Subject: I'm interested

Dominic,

Glad to hear the one-day trip from Hong Kong to Canada went well. By my sums you must have been there for a little under an hour and I think it's very much a 'well done' to you that you managed to do so much business in that time. Paul Scholes is a player who has done everything he could

----

13 See *The Dundee Courier*, 17 November 2006: *'European Football Minnows Shocked as Player Quits'*.

possibly have done in his career. If he should choose to spend his summer
holidays hanging around dressing rooms then that's fine by me.

I have parents' evening tonight at Timmy's school and will arrange
payment for the ball tomorrow.

Bob

From: Dominic Jones
To: Bob Servant
Subject: This Is Your Ball Remember

OK Bob, here again is the ball and it is ready for you now. Please let me
know right away when you send the money. Sometimes I wonder from
what I am seeing if it true you want the ball.

Dominic

From: Bob Servant
To: Dominic Jones
Subject: Penpal

Dominic,
Right, the goalposts have shifted a little here, if you'll pardon the pun. I'm
just back from parents' evening and that little bugger Timmy has fallen

seriously behind with his homework and his mum is giving me absolute dog's abuse, if you'll pardon the pun. Sometimes when she's shouting at me, Dominic, I find myself wanting to push her out a window, and that's not a pun in any way.

Anyway, one of the things Timmy's not done is a project where he was supposed to find a penpal. I was hoping you could help me out of this pickle and pony up Jerry for the job? They could have a wee chat and that would be enough and then Timmy could print off the emails and hand them in as his project.

I've promised Timmy that I'll buy him the ball as a treat as soon as he gets this done, Dominic, so let me know ASAP for all our sakes.

Yours in hope,

Bob

PS I attach a photo of the specific window that I would sometimes like to push Timmy's mum out of.

From: Dominic Jones
To: Bob Servant
Subject: Jerry's Email

Bob,
OK this is not usual but if it is needed then my son Jerry's email is
████████)@yahoo.com
   Let us get this done now please. Do not worry I understand these
problem with women we have them in our country also.

Dominic Jones.

From: Timmy Servant
To: Jerry Jones
Subject: ARE YOU MY FRIEND?

Hello Jerry!
My name is Timmy and you are my new friend. ☺ Can you tell me about
yourself? ☹ I am nine years old and I like playing football and climbing
trees. I have yellow hair and blue eyes and I live in a house with my Mum
and Dad and sometimes they shout at each other and my Dad has big
muscles like a horse.

What do you look like and what do you do?

Write back! ☺

Timmy

From: Jerry Jones
To: Timmy Servant
Subject: Yes I am Your Friend

hi,
Am Jerry Jones and am 10 years old i have black hair, blue eyes and am
living in Hong Kong with my mum and dad am i love football, basketball,
people says that i looks exactly like my dad cos he always there for me,
when i need him.

jerry.

From: Timmy Servant
To: Jerry Jones
Subject: You Are My Friend Forever

Hello Jerry!
Thank you for writing back. ☺ I love football as well I hope I will play today
after school. I wish I had black hair like the other boys. ☹ I have yellow
hair but I think it is stupid. Do you like Yellow Hair? What are you doing
today and what is your school uniform? Would you like to see my uniform?

Your Dad sounds like a bellend. ☹

Timmy

From: Jerry Jones
To: Timmy Servant
Subject: Yes friends forever now

hi,
I do not know what you mean but my Dad is a good man who looks after
his family in every way. Do not worry about your hair you have nice hair.
My uniform is jeans and a shirt yes I would like to see your uniform.
OK you can give this to your school now. Tell your dad he must buy your
football now.

jerry

From: Bob Servant
To: Dominic Jones
Subject: A bit of an awkward one

Dominic,
Timmy went out with his mother earlier and I had the opportunity to check
his email account. I'm afraid I have some rather awkward news. Timmy
and Jerry's relationship seems to have moved very quickly from two kids
messing about to something very different. I am sorry to say that they
seem to have both been overtaken by that old pal of ours: lust. Jerry
seems to be obsessed by Timmy's hair which he goes on and on about like
you wouldn't believe. He also has a 'thing' for Timmy's uniform.

Now, Dominic, I'm not against men who decide that the skirt are just
not worth the hassle. I have seven Elton John records and once bought a
full price ticket to see Ian McKellen star in a pantomime at the Dundee Rep
Theatre. (To be fair I didn't end up going because my dishwasher short-

circuited and flooded my kitchen but to blame my dishwasher problems on McKellen's sexual preferences would be unfair to both McKellen and the dishwasher so let's not go down that road.)

My point, Dominic, is this. If, when Jerry and Timmy are a little older, they still feel the same way about each other then I think we as parents should get together, have a wee drink and work out some rules. Whether or not they can have 'sleepovers' and so on. Right now they should barely be at the holding hands stage, as I'm sure you'll agree?

Bob

From: Dominic Jones
To: Bob Servant
Subject: Forget it already

This is just mad you are not real.

4

Dr Kenny Wilson

From: Kenny Wilson
To: Bob Servant
Subject: From HSBC Bank

Dear Sir,

I am the Head Manager of the HSBC Ghana bank. I would like to make an honest proposal to you. You have my personal guarantee and assurance this transaction is 100% legitimate and Risk free and under the confines of the law. I shall also require your personal Guarantee that you are someone that I can trust because I will reciprocate same to you. I would like Fund transfer of (USD$15.6 million) to you on my behalf. 40% of the fund will be for your kind assistance, 60% will be for me while we both will take care of the financial expenses of transfer of the fund into your bank account, and 10% will be for settling the expenditure.

Do not entertain any kind of fear as I will be here to give you all information which the bank will require from you. I also have a link with the Executive Governor of the HSBC Bank of Africa here, but he does not know of my involvement in this deal because it is secret. I await your urgent reply,

Best Regards,

Kenny Wilson
Head Manager HSBC Bank Ghana

From: Bob Servant
To: Kenny Wilson
Subject: RE: From HSBC Bank

Kenny Boy,
A big 'how are you doing?' from Broughty Ferry, Dundee. I'm happy with my split of the 110% and I'm glad to be involved in something that comes

to 110% because I always thought it was just something that football managers talked about.

One thing though, Big K. I know this is ridiculous, but can I just check that this isn't a scam in any way?

Your Servant,

Bob Servant

From: Kenny Wilson
To: Bob Servant
Subject: This is legitimate

Hello Bob,

Thanks for your mail, as regards your question how you would know if this transaction is genuine, well i have all the related documents to the fund intact. You can send your full account details or even come to Ghana and together we can conclude things in order. i am hoping to hear from you ASAP to proceed.

This is my personal email now. It is safer to use than the bank email. Just call me Kenny.

Regards,

Kenny Wilson

From: Bob Servant
To: Kenny Wilson
Subject: Just trying to place you?

K-bomb,

Thanks for the email. I agree that it will be far safer if we switch from the bank's Yahoo email address to your Yahoo email address. I have to say I would never have placed 'Kenny Wilson' as boxing out of Ghana. I'm a Dundee man myself and to me your name screams Glasgow and whispers Ayrshire?

Bob

From: Kenny Wilson
To: Bob Servant
Subject: My Name Is Normal

Bob

Well, that is my name and i do not think that has anything to do with business. I am a Ghanaian, i should tell you what our names are like, for your information my friend we bear names like williams, wilson, jacob, mills, woods etc

Kenny

Call me Kenny also not other ways.

From: Bob Servant
To: Kenny Wilson
Subject: Kenny It Is

Kenny (sorry for the nicknames, you don't deserve that)

   Let me make one thing as clear as ice. I was not in any way making fun of your name. I know a few Wilsons and there's not a bad guy amongst them. I remember Turn-ups Wilson, with those magnificent trousers of his, once telling me that the Dundee Wilsons are descended from Alexander the Great. Have you heard this? I have to say that, as much as I like Turn-ups, I don't think I'd let him lead me into battle!. Again, I don't mean any offence against the wider Wilson community.

   I hope all is well in Ghana and I won't do the famous 'Ghana Get You' joke out of respect to you and your family,

Bob

PS Photo attached of Turn-ups Wilson

From: Kenny Wilson
To: Bob Servant
Subject: Ok let us do the business

Bob,

About your question, i never made such inquiry to know if the wilsons
are related to Alexander the Great or not but this does not sound true. I
just want to know if you are still interested in helping me go through this
transaction. Like i said before, i have all the related documents to the
fund. Send me your banking information or come down to Ghana to meet
with me over this issue, and together we can visit the security company
where the fund is deposited to have it claimed and transferred to your
account.

Regards,

Kenny

From: Bob Servant
To: Kenny Wilson
Subject: Chappy Williams

Hi Kenny,

I share your suspicion on the Alexander The Great front and will pass on
the bad news to Turn-ups. If I may, can I also pick up on your associate
with the Williams surname? One of my best friends here in Dundee is
Chappy Williams, can you check if they're related? He lives on the estate
beside Safeways and has a slight stoop and does this thing with his eyes
when he laughs that makes it look like he's struggling to breathe. Does any
of that 'ring true' for your Williams pals?

   Although it would probably be easier if I just gave you my account
details, I'm seriously tempted by the Ghana trip for a spot of sunshine.
Would we be going to the beach? It's April here but you wouldn't have
guessed it, other than the usual April's Fool's Day fallout.[14] It's absolutely
freezing. I attach a photo of Broughty Ferry High Street taken this
afternoon.

Bob

---

14 See *The Dundee Courier*, 1 April 1 2011: *'Dundee Royal Infirmary
"Overwhelmed" by Fool's Day victims'* and *The Dundee Courier*, 2 April 2011:
'Dundee Divorce Lawyers See "Staggering' Spike". ('All I'd ask him is "Was it
really worth it?" said one middle-aged woman whose right foot had been crudely
superglued to a metal bucket').

From: Kenny Wilson
To: Bob Servant
Subject: Listen To What I Say

Hello Bob,

Thanks for the picture looks nice. Listen Bob I did not tell you that i have williams friend, i only told you that we have names like williams, wilson, mills etc, i did not say i have a friend by name williams. Secondly, i told you that when you come to meet with me in Ghana, you and i will meet with the director of the security company where the fund is deposited and have the fund claimed and transfer the total fund to your nominated bank account in your country, then i will fly to meet with you in your country for the percentage sharing,

Kenny

From: Bob Servant
To: Kenny Wilson
Subject: Eh?

Kenny,

I apologise for the Williams mix up. I'm just trying to get my head round your plan. I fly to Ghana, we sort things out there, and then we fly together back to Scotland? That's the worst plan since Gallipoli. Why don't you just send me the money?

Bob

From: Kenny Wilson
To: Bob Servant
Subject: Listen To Me

Bob,

Please we are talking about trust and a huge sum of money here sir, for me to be able to build trust completely that the fund is safe, i think it is just right that you meet with me in Ghana, we go through the process and the fund will be transferred into your bank account before i meet you in your country, it is very necessary you meet me in Ghana, it will afford you the opportunity to see the fund and to know that you are dealing with the real person, that is what i believe sir, expecting to hear from you with your arrival date and flight schedule, have a good day.

Kenny

From: Bob Servant
To: Kenny Wilson
Subject: I think I get it

Kenny,

Let's do it. I'll come to Ghana, we'll get this sorted out at the bank, have a long (and dare I say boozy?) lunch then head to the airport and fly together back to Scotland.

Any thoughts of what you want to do in Dundee? I attach a photo of the Desperate Dan statue in the city centre. It's funny to get photos taken when you each put your head in between Desperate Dan's legs and open your mouth as if to say 'Oh God I can't believe I'm doing this!'

Fancy it? It's just a bit of fun.

Bob

From: Kenny Wilson
To: Bob Servant
Subject: Book Your Flight Schedule

Hello Bob,
Thanks for your mail and for agreeing to come to Ghana to resolve this issue, i appreciate greatly and i promise you will never regret your action. Sir i do not know exactly what i will be doing in your country for now, except for my schooling which is most important to me right now and I will have to do even when in your country. The statue looks good and I am happy to visit it but not if it takes away from my schooling.

I want you to send me your flight schedule immediately.

Regards,

Kenny

From: Bob Servant
To: Kenny Wilson
Subject: School?

Kenny,
What's this school carry on? I mean, I suppose I could arrange for you to go to school while you're here but you're the main man at HSBC Ghana for Christ's sake, are you sure you need to go to school? I know the janitor at Forthill Primary School so could probably sneak you in there but you'd be a lot bigger than the other boys?

I'll fire up the Teletext now and look for flights to Ghana.

Bob

From: Kenny Wilson
To: Bob Servant
Subject: As a doctor not a school boy Bob

Hello Bob,
My schooling is that I would like to study medicine and become a
medical doctor once this is all over. This is not unusual in Ghana for
a man to go for one career and then one more. I will need to read my
medical books while I am in your country to keep me OK.

Sir have you made up your mind when you will be arriving in Ghana
for this transaction?

Regards,

Kenny

From: Bob Servant
To: Kenny Wilson
Subject: This Changes Everything

Kenny,
You're a quack? This changes everything. Dundee Royal Infirmary have
been hit hard by the cutbacks[15] and would love to have an extra pair of
hands around the place. It would be a perfect match: you'd get some
top-class experience and they'd get a free doctor who could also tell them
funny stories about managing a bank and funny things that happened
to you while you were managing the bank. That kind of stuff would be
particularly handy in the awkward moments after a patient dies.

Let me give them a call now but in the meantime start packing because
you should come here first and we can push the Ghana trip back.

Bob

From: Kenny Wilson
To: Bob Servant
Subject: Wait I am not a doctor yet

Bob I did not say I was a doctor now I said I am hoping to attend
schooling and become a doctor in the future. No you must come here first
Bob and then I will come with you to your country aftrwards. Confirm
straight away that you will do this.

---

15 See *The Dundee Courier*, 3 April 2011: *'Patients Fury at Royal Infirmary's
"Pyjama Timeshare" Scheme'*. ('"I got afternoons," complained one patient.
"Who on earth wants afternoons?"').

From: Bob Servant
To: Kenny Wilson
Subject: The Medicine Ball Is Rolling

Kenny,

Just off the phone to the hospital and it was a very positive phone call indeed. I told them you were one of the best doctors to come out of Ghana in years, that you have a bedside manner to die for (no pun intended) and you'd work for tips. I'm off up to the hospital now to hear their final offer and don't worry I'll be ticking off the major points – uniform, the lunch situation and car parking.

Bob

From: Kenny Wilson
To: Bob Servant
Subject: Do not go to the hospital

No Bob do not do this do not go to the Hospital at all. Look just send me your banking information and I will arrange this transfer for you and you do not have to come to Ghana. You must just send me $2000 to allow the transfer, OK? That is easier.

Kind Regards,

Kenny

From: Bob Servant
To: Kenny Wilson
Subject: Parking Space

Kenny,

Well that's me back from the hospital. Where to begin? I'll give you the good news first, starting with the uniform which was fine. Standard stuff, white trousers and long coat, pens in the top pocket. No problems there at all. Next up, lunch and no problems there either. Unfortunately you have to buy your own but I had a look at the canteen prices and they're heavily subsidised. I used to be in the cheeseburger van game and, believe me, no-one's getting rich off these prices.

That's the good news. The bad news, in fact the real Hiroshima news, is car parking. They told me they'd allocated you a space so I went out to the car park and from the moment I saw it something just didn't sit right with me. I don't know what kind of car you drive, Kenny, but to the naked eye your car park space looks barely usable. I have taken a photo and added a can of coke to give scope. What do you think? A bit tight?

Yours,

Bob

NO REPLY

5
Bob's Phone Number

From: Mike Christopher
To: Bob Servant
Subject: A proposal

Dear Sir/Madam,
My name is Barrister Michael Christopher, a Senior Advocate and legal consultant in practice here in the Cook Islands. My client suffered a terrible violent death life alongside with his wife in a Beirut-bound charter jet plane crashed on the Monday, 9th January 2006, 12:12 GMT (details on Internet if required).

Prior to his death my client secured a contract worth millions of US dollars from the kingdom of Bahrain. As his personal lawyer and close confidant, all my efforts to locate any of his relatives whom i can present as next of kin has proved abortive. Therefore I am seeking for your consent to present you as next of kin and subsequently the beneficiary of the fund. I will initiate this process towards a conclusion if you give me positive signals. I wait to hear from you.

Yours faithfully,

Mike Christopher

From: Bob Servant
To: Mike Christopher
Subject: You're at it!

Mike,
The Cook Islands? You must think I'm stupid. Where do you live, Frying Pan City?

Give up.

Your Servant,

Bob Servant

From: Mike Christopher
To: Bob Servant
Subject: The Cook islands

Dear Bob Servant,
What is this you are saying? The Cook Islands are recognised province.
Do you want to act as next of kin? The commission is very kind.

Yours faithfully,

Mike Christopher

From: Bob Servant
To: Mike Christopher
Subject: I hold my hands up

Barrister Christopher,
I have just had a look at my atlas and would like to apologise, as the Red
Indians say, 'with reservations'.[16] I accept that the Cook Islands exist but
I am also nervous about meeting new people from the Internet. I am an
elderly man and also have a good few quid (don't tell the wife!) (I don't
have a wife) and this makes me a target for likely lads and chancers such
as this bunch below. They might be housewives' favourites, Christopher,
but they're naughty with it![17]

Yours,

Bob

---

16 This is one of Bob's favourite jokes but has always struck me as a little obtuse.
I once probed him at a corner table in Broughty Ferry's Stewpot's Bar on how
exactly this selection of words operate as a joke. He replied, 'A lot of people
like Rolls Royces but do they know what's under the bonnet?' I answered that
yes, those same people would be aware that under the bonnet of a Rolls Royce
would be a Rolls Royce engine. Bob replied by asking if I thought the table had
'a wobble'. I replied that it didn't. Bob then spent five minutes frowning and
wobbling the table with his hand before leaving for a lengthy bathroom visit.
17 Along with this email Bob sent three photos to demonstrate suitable
'housewives' favourites'. The photos were of David Jason in character as Del Boy,
Ian McShane in character as Lovejoy and Osama bin Laden in character as Osama
bin Laden. Unfortunately I cannot include the photos here as one of those three
'likely lads' refused permission (to be fair, it wasn't bin Laden who did not cause
the production of this book any problems at all).

From: Mike Christopher
To: Bob Servant
Subject: A proposal

Dear Mr Servant,
Yes I understand your worries but do not worry in this case because I am a Barrister of course so this is legal and just. This is excellent Bob and I can confirm you are now the front runner to be the main beneficiary of this will minus our administration fees which as normal will have to be paid first. They are very low, only $200, OK?

Yours faithfully,

Mike Christopher

From: Bob Servant
To: Mike Christopher
Subject: Phone

Barrister Mike,
$200 is a drop in the bloody ocean. During Dundee's Cheeseburger Wars I'd earn that much by putting my shoes on and the same again for brushing my hair.
    Listen, It might be quicker to talk over the phone. Would you mind calling me?

Yours,

Bob

From: Mike Christopher
To: Bob Servant
Subject: I will call

Yes of course I will call you at my expense Bob just send the number

----

From: Bob Servant
To: Mike Christopher
Subject: Phone Number

OK are you ready?

From: Mike Christopher
To: Bob Servant
Subject: Give me the number

Yes I am ready.

From: Bob Servant
To: Mike Christopher
Subject: Here we go

0

From: Mike Christopher
To: Bob Servant
Subject: RE: Here we go

Hello Bob I think that did not come through please send it again.

From: Bob Servant
To: Mike Christopher
Subject: RE: Here we go

0

From: Mike Christopher
To: Bob Servant
Subject: Not coming through

That did not come through again sorry Bob please send again.

From: Bob Servant
To: Mike Christopher
Subject: Seems fine my end

4

From: Mike Christopher
To: Bob Servant
Subject: Not right

Bob this is not correct I am not getting the full number please check that you are sending it.

From: Bob Servant
To: Mike Christopher
Subject: RE: Not right

4

From: Mike Christopher
To: Bob Servant
Subject: RE: Not right

Bob what is this? You are not sending your number properly I am only getting one number through a 0 and now 4s what is this?

From: Bob Servant
To: Mike Christopher
Subject: Eh?

I don't quite understand your problem, I'm sending it through. 0044 is the code for the UK. Next bit:

1

From: Mike Christopher
To: Bob Servant
Subject: Send the whole number

What are you saying to me Bob? You're sending me the number one at every time? Why would you do this Bob just send the whole thing.

From: Bob Servant
To: Mike Christopher
Subject: Security

Mike,
As I told you I am worried about Internet security. Please give me the respect I deserve.

3

From: Mike Christopher
To: Bob Servant
Subject: RE: Security

This is too stupid but OK. 004413 come on

From: Bob Servant
To: Mike Christopher
Subject: 8

From: Mike Christopher
To: Bob Servant
Subject: Got it

0044138 OK more

From: Bob Servant
To: Mike Christopher
Subject: 2

From: Mike Christopher
To: Bob Servant
Subject: More needed

00441382 more

From: Bob Servant
To: Mike Christopher
Subject: 2

From: Mike Christopher
To: Bob Servant
Subject: send the rest now

004413822 more

From: Bob Servant
To: Mike Christopher
Subject: 2

From: Mike Christopher
To: Bob Servant
Subject: RE: 2

0044138222 more

From: Bob Servant
To: Mike Christopher
Subject: Hang on

Sorry I've lost my thread a bit. I think I've gone a bit heavy on the 2s.
Would you mind reading back what I've sent so far?

From: Mike Christopher
To: Bob Servant
Subject: OK here

0044138222 send the rest.

From: Bob Servant
To: Mike Christopher
Subject: Remember the security!

Sorry, can you send it one number at a time? It's safer.

From: Mike Christopher
To: Bob Servant
Subject: RE: Remember the security!

Are you serious?

From: Bob Servant
To: Mike Christopher
Subject: Good Question

What do you think? (be honest)

From: Mike Christopher
To: Bob Servant
Subject: RE: Good Question

FUCK you if this is not true

From: Bob Servant
To: Mike Christopher
Subject: RE: Good Question

4

NO REPLY

6

The War at Home

My name is Sergeant Gary Kaltwesser. I am a trusted operator in the US Army Marines and currently on deployment here in Afghanistan. I am from Illinios and have 19 years service. We are under constant attack here and I am able to get on only when things are not wild but I saw your profile and thought we could have a connection.

Please dear tell me of your life and I will tell you of yours.

Your Sergeant Gary

From: Bob Servant
To: Sergeant Gary Kaltwesser
Subject: Morning Sarge

Sergeant Gary,
Thanks so much for dropping me a wee line from the trenches. It's wonderful to hear from a military man, and I will tell you right now that I'm firmly behind the troops. At the end of the day you lads are just doing your jobs and if a few heads get knocked together along the way then so be it.

It's also great to hear that the Afghanistan gig is still going. I know that the Iraq roadshow got wrapped up last year and it's an open secret that the boo boys reckon both Afghanistan and Iraq have been shite wars because of the lack of major surprises and the time difference.

Well, I've not given up on Afghanistan and I'm delighted to hear that you haven't either, Gary. We've not had a good war since the Falklands and I still think there are a couple of wee twists in the Afghanistan tale yet.

Keep your head down pal.

Your Servant,

Bob Servant

From: Sergeant Gary Kaltwesser
To: Bob Servant
Subject: Hello there

Hey There,
Thanks for taking the time to respond, makes me feel we've got a connection already. I will love to tell you more about me it's just that I don't always get to log on there to chat. You'll need to know that I'm serving the US Army Marines and currently on deployment here in Afghanistan. I am from Illinios and have served 19 active years with different infantry units.

I have been to a bunch of hot spots around the world and continue to do so today. I generally socialize outside of the military community since I'm single and my peers are pretty much all married with children. I am an avid athlete, having played most sports at one time or another – everything from Adventure racing to Wiffle ball! Someday I'll move home and be able to surf, paddle and dive like I love to do.

Write back soon dear,

Sergeant Gary Kaltwesser

From: Bob Servant
To: Sergeant Gary Kaltwesser
Subject: Hello there

Sergeant Gary,
What a life you've had, pitching up in the world's hot spots looking all smart
in your uniform. I get nervous driving through Dundee's troubled West
Ferry estate[18] so I can only imagine what it's like there in Afghanistan.
Even popping out to the shops or heading uptown to look for skirt must be
a real ball-ache.

   Oh Gary, I hope more than anything that one day you'll be paddling like
you used to. And, if you'll have me, I'll be paddling right there beside you.

Fully naked.

Bob

From: Sergeant Gary Kaltwesser
To: Bob Servant
Subject: This is what I want also

Bob,
Thank you and yes we will be together in this way. I want you to know
am a man of one woman, I treat my woman with respect and care.
Am a caring man, who show my woman what true love means, i work
according to word of God. I'm a romantic man, I love going to the beach,
listen to musics, love taking a walk, love going to the cinemas. I would
describe myself as very caring a gentle and positive person.

   I had like to meet a woman who is caring and considerate, someone
I can trust and who will trust me and will always be honest with
me, someone who enjoys laughing at the silly things that happen in
life. Someone who is willing to share the work to make our home a
comfortable place. Someone who likes to live in a tidy house too, I do not
like to have things very messy.

What do you seek in your ideal man?

Your Soldier Man

Sgt. Gary Kaltwesser

---

18 See *The Dundee Courier*, 16 February 2006: '*Council Berated For Poverty
"Celebration"*' ('Dundee City Council were forced to defend themselves last night
after marking the West Ferry estate's inclusion in an EU document highlighting
inner-city poverty with a drinks reception. "At the end of the day a European title
is just that," said a council spokesman. "We've put Dundee in the spotlight and on
the lips of the Brussels top dogs. If anything, we should be applauded."')

From: Bob Servant
To: Sergeant Gary Kaltwesser
Subject: My Ideal Man

Gary,

Great question. My ideal man would have a decent line in jokes, just under my ability would probably work best, and should always let me finish what I'm saying before having a wee crack at something himself. Also, I don't like when men sometimes use their wives and families as an easy excuse to get out of things like sleepovers and I can't bear the ones that clasp their hands behind their backs and sort of rock on their feet while they speak. It's a cheap way of gaining control over a conversation and I will not have it. Not on my watch.

Hope that helps,

Bob

From: Sergeant Gary Kaltwesser
To: Bob Servant
Subject: Hello Darling

Hi Hun,

How are you doing today? This is the man I am! it is like a dream that we have found each other. The woman I will end up with will love to spend time with me but also have her own life. We will share popcorn at an early matinee, search for treasures at local garage sales and touch, feel and squeeze the vegetables at a road side produce stand. She will be a perfect lady in public and our time behind closed doors will be natural and giving. She will be my life. I will be her 'rock'.

I will send her roses for no particular reason, with notes like 'Thank you for being in my life'. She will never doubt my feelings for her. She will become accustom to me mouthing the words 'I love you' across a crowded room. She will know how I feel about her. I will love, protect and guide her. I am looking for a lover, companion, friend and wife. Let the passion begin. i have butterflies running in my stomach now, i have never feel this way before.

Gary

From: Bob Servant
To: Sergeant Gary Kaltwesser
Subject: Release the butterflies Gary

Gary,

There seems to have been a bit of confusion. I am a 64-year-old man from

Dundee's celebrated Broughty Ferry estate here in Scotland. I hope that information allows you to lie back, open your mouth and let the butterflies fly away unharmed.

Having said that I have no problem at all with squeezing the odd vegetable, mouthing stuff across crowded rooms and sending each other notes. However, if we were to do that then I'd rather we were mouthing 'Isn't this room crowded?' and the notes said 'How's tricks? Fancy watching Zulu at mine on Saturday morning?'

I thought we were going to be friends and talk about Army stuff but there seems to have been a terrible mix-up.

Bob

From: Sergeant Gary Kaltwesser
To: Bob Servant
Subject: So Sorry

OMG . . . am so sorry about all this, i also met a woman online and i thought she was the one that has been mailing me. You said about naked and I thought that meant you were a women. Anyways it's okay we can always be friend. Tell me more about you my friend and yes what do you need to hear on life in the Army.

Gary

From: Bob Servant
To: Sergeant Gary Kaltwesser
Subject: Army

Gary,

Don't worry about getting it horribly wrong on the skirt front because I know how that feels. My pals will probably write 'He got it horribly wrong on the skirt front' on my gravestone. They probably would too, the terrible bastards.

My Army questions are really just the ones you must get all the time:

How big is your gun?

Have you ever killed anyone?

Can you do a forward roll while running? What I mean by that is would you have to stop running and do the forward roll or could you go straight from running into the forward roll?

All the best,

Bob

From: Sergeant Gary Kaltwesser
To: Bob Servant
Subject: RE: Army

Hi Bob,

Yes I have a gun like all Marines. We have different guns for different situations. We don't just shoot anyhow or anybody but i have shot 4 bad men on their leg while trying to run off to explosive area and some passed away but they are all bad Muslim and corrupted people. Yes I think I could do run and roll as this is the kind of thing we train to do Bob.

I can't talk too great right now. We are short of troops and also we got trapped in the desert where mines were everywhere so we have to go back inside the Capital until the whole mines was taking out. It's seriously messy out here for now Bob. We also ran out of ammo until the rush team came in and help us out. It is just for the grace of God that kept us all alive.

Have been hearing about the situation in Libya, please my friend tell me some more.

Your good friend,

Gary

From: Bob Servant
To: Sergeant Gary Kaltwesser
Subject: Bad Times

Gary,

Good to hear from you and sorry to hear things are getting so hairy. I'm glad you can do the run and roll and I strongly suggest you use it the next time you're in a pickle. It's a move that catches people seriously off guard. I used it at Dundee train station a few weeks ago in an attempt to get past the new barriers they've put in. Although I failed to get past the barriers, and was knocked out for fifteen minutes, the major reaction from the punters was an intense respect.[19]

I'm having my own problems over here just now, Gary. Broughty Ferry Bowling Club are holding their elections and I've thrown my hat in the ring as Social Secretary. I should be an absolute shoo-in for the role but there's a guy Archie standing against me and he's got the ear of the committee. I'm trying to find out what's going on and will keep you posted.

Keep running pal,

Bob

---

19 See *The Dundee Courier*, 29 March 2011: *'Station Management Slam "Kamikaze" Fare-dodger'*.

PS No idea on Libya, the Dundee Courier aren't big on foreign news.[20] I do however know of the boy Gaddafi because of the famous rhyme –

> If you're going to a cafe
> Don't invite Gaddafi

From: Sergeant Gary Kaltwesser
To: Bob Servant
Subject: Hello

My Friend,
Thank you for telling me about your life. It sounds like this club of yours has people with closed minds. This is not what I believe. I believe in freedom and this was one of the reasons I took this path. Now here in Afghanistan I am just trying to make this job work for my country and the people. It is not easy. Lots of civilians are innocent but there is corrupt suicide bombers and others who would shoot me and my men first chance comes their way.

What is tough Bob is not having the right provisions. I have food and shelter but I can always do with just a little extra for things like cigarettes and maybe some candy and things like this. Do you think as a friend you could send some money maybe just a little? $500 would make my life so much easier here for times when we are not under direct attack.

Gary

From: Bob Servant
To: Sergeant Gary Kaltwesser
Subject: RE: Hello

Gary,
No problem at all, I will send you some cigarettes, a large bag of fun-sized Milky Ways and some spare military hardware in the form of an intimidating costume (photo attached). What's the best address for you in Afghanistan?

Bob

---

20 See *The Dundee Courier*, 18 June 1939, p. 27: '*Moustachioed German Invades "Poland"*'.

From: Sergeant Gary Kaltwesser
To: Bob Servant
Subject: Hi

My Friend,
Thank you so much for your kindness. I cannot accept packages because
we are always on the move and no-one must know where I am so the
money is best. Thank you for this Bob I will think of my Scotland friend
Bob when I have my rest days and can relax properly with my cigarrates
and candy.

Are you OK to send it today by Western Union?

True friend

Gary

From: Bob Servant
To: Sergeant Gary Kaltwesser
Subject: The Bowling Club

Gary,
It's all kicking off up the bowling club. I was up there earlier and the
atmosphere could poison a shark. No-one is looking anyone in the eye and

Archie is swaggering about the place like Eric Bristow on a stag do. I don't like this Gary, I don't like it all.

Will report back soon Gary. Over and out.

Bob

From: Sergeant Gary Kaltwesser
To: Bob Servant
Subject: Do not forget the money

Bob,
Sorry to hear this you should ask about and get the true situation that is my main advice.

Did you get my note about sending the money?

Gary

From: Bob Servant
To: Sergeant Gary Kaltwesser
Subject: Bugs?

Gary,
Well it's as we expected. Archie's apparently sown up the committee. They're having a meeting tomorrow night and it sounds like he's going to get rubber stamped through. This is unbelievable, Gary. I thought Britain was a democracy but apparently I was wrong. You were talking the other day about Libya. Well if that boy Gaddafi is run out of Libya then he should get himself along to Broughty Ferry Bowling Club because that mob would probably make him captain. It used to be run by good lads like Bill Wood and Jimmy Walker and it's heartbreaking to see it like this.

I was thinking about heading back up there and hanging about outside the President's window. Could you give me some military advice please, Gary? A lot of the time in films you will see people using 'bugs'. Where can I get a bug and when I have hidden the bug how do I go about hearing the thing? Through a Walkman?

On second thoughts the bug plan sounds quite complicated. Would it be easier if you just taught me, over email, how to lip read?

Bob

From: Sergeant Gary Kaltwesser
To: Bob Servant
Subject: Yes I can help

Hello Bob

You are having luck because I have 5 years experience in this field.
First let me say please this should be confidential what i mean by saying
confidential is that it should be strictly private just between you and me
only so as not to jeopardies my life and my job.

For tapping in with a bug this can be done easily. I can give you an
arrangement to buy one and tell you how to go about this. The right bug
can be heard for 50 meters all around. I will show you how to use this
when you buy it. this would be best Bob for you to buy a bug through
me because for reading lips well this is very hard. Of course I can teach
you from my experience but it would take a long time and is different for
every language.

Your friend

Gary

From: Bob Servant
To: Sergeant Gary Kaltwesser
Subject: Just Back

Gary,

Unfortunately your email didn't arrive in time. I went up to the bowling
club and had a look in the window but it was a complete washout. I tried
to lipread but the only word I could make out was 'super-injunction' so
I presume that was just part of the topical smalltalk at the beginning.
The only reason I picked up that one was because the hyphen makes it
obvious, but other than that I was stumped.

What I can say is the two of them were getting on great guns. Lots of
laughing and stuff with the eyes that very clearly said 'we are friends and
this is fun'.

I've heard on the grapevine they're having one more meeting tomorrow
Gary so that's my last chance. I'm going to head up with my neighbour
Frank and have it out with them. I need advice from you in the morning, are
you available?

Hope you're having a fun night. I'm shattered so right now for me it's a
pie, a pint, pyjamas and bed. The three P's. And a B.

Cheers,

Bob

From: Sergeant Gary Kaltwesser
To: Bob Servant
Subject: Yes I can help

Hello Bob
I hope you slept well. I am having a bit of rest time. We have been in the battle field last night and it was crazy there Bob. Now I have a week away from the madness. Can you send the $500 by Western Union today so I can buy the cigarettes and candy?

If you send the money I can give you the best advice you will get for this problem at your club.

Your friend

Gary

From: Bob Servant
To: Sergeant Gary Kaltwesser
Subject: Waterboarding?

Morning Gary,
I was up with the birds this morning. Which is only fair, I had to sort out their taxis and so on.[21]

Right, let's get cracking. Here's the plan. The bowling club is shut today but I know the president will be in there getting everything set up for the election later. So me and Frank are going to head up and have it out with him. What I need from you Gary is interrogation tactics. I need to be able to get inside his head, how do I do that? And if he doesn't talk how can I make him? Frank was saying his nephew was telling him about something called 'waterboarding' that the Americans have been going nuts for. Anything in that?

Bob

From: Sergeant Gary Kaltwesser
To: Bob Servant
Subject: I know this

Bob
Waterboarding yeah this is something that we have to doo from time to time to get what we need from the bad Muslim we catch in the field. Its

---

21 Another of Bob's favourite jokes. I would estimate that I have heard it over 400 times but have to concede this is considerably less than Bob's desperately unfortunate postman.

real easy Bob but best for now you send me the money before you go up to the club and then we can talk more. OK?

Gary

From: Bob Servant
To: Sergeant Gary Kaltwesser
Subject: SHOW TIME

GARY ON WAY TO BOWLING CLUB FRANK IS IN A TRACKSUIT AND I HAVE ALL THE STUFF FOR THE WATERBOARDING ROGER OVER AND OUT FOXTROT

Sent from my BlackBerry® wireless device[22]

From: Sergeant Gary Kaltwesser
To: Bob Servant
Subject: Western Union

OK Bob but go to the Western Union on the way and send my money.

From: Bob Servant
To: Sergeant Gary Kaltwesser
Subject: GAME ON

HAVE STRIPPED PRESIDENT NAKED HE IS LYING ON THE FLOOR AND I AM ABOUT TO FIX THE HOSE TO HIS MOUTH

Sent from my BlackBerry® wireless device

From: Sergeant Gary Kaltwesser
To: Bob Servant
Subject: Do not do this

Wait BOB. This is not right. Stop what you are doing. Clean up this mess with the man and go

----

From: Bob Servant
To: Sergeant Gary Kaltwesser
Subject: RE: Do not do this

HE'S FILLING UP LIKE A FUCKING BALLOON

Sent from my BlackBerry® wireless device

---

22 Bob Servant owns no BlackBerry.

From: Sergeant Gary Kaltwesser
To: Bob Servant
Subject: Stop it

What The Hell is now going on?

From: Bob Servant
To: Sergeant Gary Kaltwesser
Subject: RE: Stop it

IT'S ALL GONE SHITCAKES GARY. I'M OFF

Sent from my BlackBerry® wireless device

From: Sergeant Gary Kaltwesser
To: Bob Servant
Subject: RE: Stop it

What is it?

From: Sergeant Gary Kaltwesser
To: Bob Servant
Subject: Speak to me Bob

Hello Bob,
I did not hear from you yesterday. Are you there? Hope all now OK with
this club and you can go to a Western Union?

Waiting to hear

Gary

From: DI Lansbury
To: Sergeant Gary Kaltwesser
Subject: Your Assistance Required

Good Afternoon,
I am a Detective Inspector at Dundee Police Station and am investigating
the murder of a local bowling club president. Right now, the case is still
very unclear but it appears that he was inflated with water until the point of
what the pathologist is calling 'disintegration'.

My prime suspect is a man called Robert Servant. He is pleading
his innocence and says that at the time of the murder he was 'up a tree'.

However we have now accessed his computer and I see you are the last person he had contact with.

Can you please explain the exact nature of your relationship with Mr Servant?

Yours,

Detective Inspector Angela Lansbury
Dundee Police Force

No 'problem' too small!

NO REPLY

7
Why Me? 2

Hello dear,

My name is Rose. I am 24 years old and am residing in the refugee camp in Sudan as a result of the civil war in my country. Please listen to this important information, My late father was the managing director of a major Factory and he was the personal advicer to the former head of state before the rebels attacked our house and killed my mother and my father in cold blood. It was only me that is alive now and I managed to make my way to this camp.

When my father was alive he deposited money in one of the leading banks in Europe which he used my name as the next of kin. The amount in question is $9.3 (Nine Million three Hundred Thousand US Dollars). And i have contacted the bank so that i can have the money to start a new life but they requested that i should have a foreign partner as my representative due to my living status here. I know that you would be a proper person for this. I know already that I trust you. I need only your information.

Yours in love.

Rose

From: Bob Servant
To: Rose
Subject: RE: Why Me?

Rose,

Great to hear from you again. You appear to have sent me exactly the same email you sent me a couple of months ago so I am sorry to hear that things have not improved at your end. However, I'm disappointed to see that your $9.3m has not gained any interest in the meantime. I'm no expert, but an amount that large should really be on a decent interest rate. Anyway, things are progressing OK at my end with the book. I've met some great colleagues of yours in the Internet cowboy game and am just about to speak to some more.

As I said, you're more than welcome to get involved?

Your Servant,

Bob Servant

From: Rose
To: Bob Servant
Subject: RE: Why Me?

I remember you I told you I have no time. Yes this is the same email because things have not got better for me in the refugee camp if you have time to write a book then you should have time to help people in my situation but maybe you are just selfish man then OK fine I will find people with God in their lives because every day I fight just to get enough to eat.

From: Bob Servant
To: Rose
Subject: RE: Why Me?

Rose,
OK, again that's your decision not to appear in the book and once again I will fully respect it.

If I may give one quick piece of advice it would be that, if you're really hungry, I would consider selling your laptop.

Yours in trust,

Bob

NO REPLY

8

Twinklers

From: Financial Services
To: Bob Servant
Subject: Loan Available Now!

Do you need a loan for business or personal use? If yes contact us

----

From: Bob Servant
To: Financial Services
Subject: In The Nick Of Time

A big 'Dundee hello' to the world famous 'Financial Services'!

Thanks for getting in touch. I need some readies badly. Can you Geldof me up?[23]

Your Servant,

Bob Servant

From: Peter Smith
To: Bob Servant
Subject: Application

Mr Servant
Thanks for your mail. I want you to fill the information required for the processing of the loan request. Interest rate is 3% per annum. We put our

----

23 Bob uses Geldof both as verb and noun. 'Geldof me up', is a request for payment, while 'Are you Geldoffed?' or 'Have you got any Geldof?' are interchangeable queries as to whether someone possesses money. See also his use of Mugabe. 'He got Mugabe'd' can mean that someone has been: beaten up, robbed or become heavily intoxicated, whereas 'He's having a Mugabe' has, in my experience, solely meant that someone is enjoying a day of good fortune at the bookmakers. If I had the time, and you the patience, I would similarly cover Bob's multiple uses of 'Alegiah' and 'Corbett'.

client interest first in our transaction and we promise to give you our best possible in this transaction.

FILL THE BORROWER'S INFORMATION BELOW:

Your Name:
Your Address:
Your Country:
Your Occupation:
Sex/Age:
Loan Amount Needed:
Loan Duration:
Monthly Income:
Cell Phone Number:

Have a nice day and God Bless you.

Best Regards,

Peter Smith
Financial Services

From: Bob Servant
To: Peter Smith
Subject: Quick Question

Peter,

Thanks for getting in touch, it's nice to hear from the organ grinder directly. I think it's fantastic that you're lending out readies and Geldoffing up the people because it's dark times round our way, Peter, what with the recession and all.

The Broughty Ferry branch of the Bank of Scotland has even cancelled fancy dress Fridays because it was hitting the wrong note.[24] Not before time to be honest, Peter, I've heard some horror stories. The boys from Berkeley's Butchers went in with their redundancy cheques and were served by a six foot tall Noel Edmonds, while my neighbour Frank got turned down for a remortgage by Freddie Mercury which was a blow for him financially and has given him some awful nightmares.

So well done to Financial Services and yourself personally for stepping into the breach. Can I just check, are there any rules about what the loan

---

24 See *The Dundee Courier*, 3 March, 2011: *'No More Fancy Dress at Broughty Bank'* ('"The public spoke and we've listened," said branch manager Gordon Smart, from within a pantomime cow.')

has to be for? And you don't have a branch in Dundee do you? That would save on the legwork.

Bob

From: Peter Smith
To: Bob Servant
Subject: Application Form

Hello Bob,
I looked up Dundee in Scotland. This is a long way from us bob. We are based in the Financial Center here in Singapore. We also operate in India. We give out loans to all kinds of people, firms, school, churches and industries. So there are not rules for the loan purpose do not worry.

We are certified, trustworthy and reliable. Just send your personal information to begin. The form is attached again.

Our Address for your records Bob

Registered Company Name: Standard Alliance Loans international, Inc.

RC No: 04589

Office Address: ████████████████████████████████████, New Delhi

Telephone Number: ████████████

Best Regards,

Peter Smith
Financial Services

From: Bob Servant
To: Peter Smith
Subject: OK

Peter,
OK, here's my full plan for the loan. I want to start a magazine called Twinklers. What kind of magazine will Twinklers be? Hold tight and I'll tell you. Twinklers will exclusively feature amateur models with particularly twinkly eyes. You simply do not get anything better in life, Peter, than a decent set of twinkly eyes. Wogan built a career on it and he wasn't the only one: look at the Queen Mum, Des Lynam or Fatima Whitbread. But I won't be pulling in any big guns like that. I want to find fresh meat, local talent from the streets of Dundee. I'm going to trawl through the bars

with Frank and his disposable camera and find some top-level twinklers, then stick their mugs in the magazine and get it out there.

Now, I know what your worry might be here, Peter. You're probably wondering if this is jazz mag territory. Well I can assure you right now, with my hand on my liver, that it is nothing of the sort. Look Peter, I'm not naive. I know that for a certain type of weirdo a nice set of twinklers might be right up their street in a jazz mag sense but you can't blame me for that. I'm selling them the bullets, I'm not asking them to fire their guns.

Bob

From: Peter Smith
To: Bob Servant
Subject: This is OK

Bob,
This is quite confusing but you are saying you will start a magazine with the loan? This is OK. All is OK, just send the information.

Peter Smith
Financial Services

From: Bob Servant
To: Peter Smith
Subject: We're talking ten

Peter,
Thanks for giving Twinklers the nod. I have set things in motion over here. I just went and chanced my arm with Inky Edwards. Inky, as you may be aware, has the big newsagents on the Dundee Road, and what that guy doesn't know about the magazine game isn't worth knowing.

Inky was good enough to give me a few minutes and I told him all about Twinklers and the hopes that you and I have for it. I'll put you out your misery straight away, Peter: Inky loved it. He reckons he's good for ten copies and we could sell them for a fiver each. So that's £50 coming in as sales so, by my calculations, we should therefore spend about £10,000 on putting the magazine together.

So I hereby request £10,000 from you Peter. That's right, ten large. Ten bags of sand.

Bob
Editor
Twinklers Magazine

From: Peter Smith
To: Bob Servant
Subject: Approved

Bob,
I have good news, your application for £10,000 has been fully approved by the board. We think that this magazine will be a success and we trust you and believe your character is good.

Therefore we need just the application in full,

Thank you and congratulations on your loan.

Peter Smith
Financial Services

From: Bob Servant
To: Peter Smith
Subject: Slogan

Peter,
I'm getting on with the form. A quick one in the meantime, how about this for a slogan for the mag:

Twinklers: Putting A Twinkle in Your Day and a Winkle in Your Way!

Thoughts?

Bob

From: Peter Smith
To: Bob Servant
Subject: Fine

Bob,
That is a good idea it will help get attention. We are impressed with you Bob and the loan is yours as soon as we have the form.

Peter

From: Bob Servant
To: Peter Smith
Subject: It's not really working for me

Pedro,

I've had a good look at the slogan you suggested. To be honest, I can't quite follow what you're getting at. What do you actually mean by 'a Winkle in Your Way'? Maybe I'm missing the joke but to me it sounds like gibberish?

Bob

From: Peter Smith
To: Bob Servant
Subject: That was you not me

Bob,

I never suggested this saying it was you do not remember? I did not think it was sense either but did not say from respect for you. Now Bob where is the form?

Peter

From: Bob Servant
To: Peter Smith
Subject: Early Contenders

Peter,

Phew, I'm glad you agree we need to scrap your slogan. That could have been a really awkward one and really it's a 'well done' to you for holding your hands up and admitting you'd sold me a pup. I'm going to stick with Twinklers: Putting a Twinkle in Your Day!

Now, Peter. Frank and I went out last night on our first twinklers hunt and I think we've come up with a few early contenders for the first issue. As the executive editor, we'll obviously be guided by you. So can you just pick out your top three?

As soon as you do that I'll get my info to you,

Yours,

Bob Servant
Editor, Twinklers Magazine: Putting a Twinkle in Your Day!

From: Peter Smith
To: Bob Servant
Subject: What is this?

Bob,
What are you doing? I do not want to be direct involved in your magazine Bob. However if needed I will pick the pretty girl and the man in the hat. Now see your side of bargain right Bob I have done my job more than enough.

Peter

From: Bob Servant
To: Peter Smith
Subject: Dogs?

Peter,
Had a bit of a brainwave. How about 'Pet's Corner' where people can submit photos of any pets that they reckon have a decent pair of twinklers? I went out with Frank and got some samples from the dog mob. Would you mind picking the first entry for Pet's Corner?

The form is nearly done,

Bob

From: Peter Smith
To: Bob Servant
Subject: OK

Bob,
Well Bob only 2 of them are real dogs which you must know. I will say the dog with white hair it looks fun.

I am starting to wonder what you are doing here Bob. I am the manager of the loan company I do not have responsibility to help you with the magazine itself.

SEND THE INFORMATION RIGHT NOW Bob

Peter

From: Bob Servant
To: Peter Smith
Subject: A Walk On The Wild Side?

Peter,
I had a little think. When wild animals are tamed they tend to lose a bit of twinkle from their eyes, just look at Moby Dick or George Best. So instead of domestic pets, why don't we 'take a walk on the wild side'?

To that end Frank and I headed up to Dundee's famous Ninewells Zoo earlier this afternoon. It's just reopened after that nonsense about the wardens being too pally with the animals.[25] Anyway, we got some shots below.

---

25 See *The Dundee Courier*, 13 March 2011: *'Zoo Apologises for "Over-friendly" Wardens'* ('The director of Dundee's Camperdown Zoo apologised today after it was revealed that a number of wardens had been befriending the animals in their care. One warden was reported to have regularly visited the nearby Odeon cinema with a chimpanzee while a senior warden has resigned after it emerged he went on holiday to Ibiza with an ostrich. "The wardens have been spoken to," said Zoo Director Steven Godden. "The otter is healthy and other than a couple of minor issues, so is the ostrich." Under further questioning, Godden admitted that the ostrich is suffering from sunburn and now bears a tattoo reading "Boys on Tour, Ibiza 2011, No Limits".')

What do you think? Do you see a cover star amongst them?

Bob

Editor, Twinklers Magazine: Putting a Twinkle in Your Day!

From: Peter Smith
To: Bob Servant
Subject: Have heard enough

Bob Servant,
I am losing trust in you now. I know you are wanting to do this magazine with the eyes and now the animals but Bob this is not my job. I am only arranging the loan.

Where is your personal information? This has been promised by you for so long it is just not right.

What are you doing?

Peter Smith
Financial Services

From: Bob Servant
To: Peter Smith
Subject: The Worst Possible News

Peter,

I just had a pretty awful meeting with Inky Edwards. I told him what we've been up to, and how you wanted to push the animal angle, and the guy looked at me like I had two noses.

To cut a long story short, Inky is withdrawing his support for Twinklers. He says that when he first heard of the idea he was all for it because he liked the fact that with all the council cutbacks we were going to support local folk through giving them work modelling their twinklers for the magazine. But he said we've lost our way with the animal thing because that is not helping the local unemployed. As Inky said, and it was hard to argue with him, 'no-one's ever sacked a penguin'.

With the loss of Inky's order, Peter, I have zero customers. With the best will in the world, you can't run a business without customers. You'll know what I mean by that. I'm afraid the game's up and I just don't know what else to say, Peter. I feel like Rory Bremner is throwing darts at my balls while talking like John Major. Again, you'll know what I mean by that.

Your Servant,

Bob Servant
Former Editor of Twinklers Magazine: Putting a Twinkle in Your Day!

From: Peter Smith
To: Bob Servant
Subject: final option

Send the information today or you forget about the loan

9
Sad Times Publishing 1

From: Mary Riley
To: Bob Servant
Subject: Can you help?

Dearly Beloved,
My name is Mrs. Mary Riley and I write this to you through my tears
of sorrow. I am a dying woman who has decided to donate what I have
to charity through you. You may be wondering why I chose you. But
someone has to be chosen. I am 66 years old and have been touched by
the lord to donate from what I have inherited from my late husband to
charity through you for the good work of humanity. I had good parents
who died and now i am careful to stop my husband's bad relatives from to
use his hard earned funds inappropriately.

I have asked the lord to forgive me all my sins and I believe he has,
because He is merciful. You no idea that problems I have had in my life.
It has been so hard from the very start and now I want to
give the sum of (GBP 8 Million) to charity through you for the good work
of the lord, and to help the motherless, less privileged and also for the
assistance of the widows.

76

At the moment I cannot take any telephone calls, due to the fact that I have been restricted by my doctor from taking telephone calls because I deserve all the rest I can get. Please contact my lawyer with your details though the details attach.

Yours in trust,
Mary Riley

From: Bob Servant
To: Mary Riley
Subject: Quick one

Mary,
Ever thought of writing a book?

Your Servant,

Bob Servant
Managing Editor
Sad Times Publishing

From:Mary Riley
To: Bob Servant
Subject: Re: Quick one

What do you mean by this? Have you contacted my lawyer as the plan?

From: Bob Servant
To: Mary Riley
Subject: Sad Times Publishing

Mary,
Wipe your tears away my friend because I have some news that I think will lift your chin right up into the clouds. Mary, I am the Managing Editor of a Scottish publisher called Sad Times Publishing. We're largely looking for stories like yours, real weepies that will reach into our reader's bodies through their eyes and play merry hell with their hearts. They're called misery memoirs over here, Mary, and we've been behind all the big Scottish ones in recent years such as –

Black, Blue and Hungry Too – The Terrible Story of Jimmy Krankie

Please Dad, Not the Face! – The Awful Life of Andrew Marr

and

I Just Need(ed) a Friend – How the pop band Texas escaped a life of poverty and pick pocketing to top the music charts.

Mary, I think your story would fit very comfortably indeed into our wee collection. Are you on board? Will you 'lift the biro' for Sad Times Publishing?

Yours,

Bob Servant
Managing Editor
Sad Times Publishing

From: Mary Riley
To: Bob Servant
Subject: Payment

Bob,
Yes I can tell you my terrible story that will be like this others that you have. Please Bob I will tell you my story and now can maybe an advance payment to be helpful my dear? I took it upon myself as a challenge to God that i must fulfill a charity deed in life. There are more you don't know about me and If you agree with me to have my full story you will have to do what i have requested. What is the pay? It will boost my charity giving.

 Whenever I think about my life I cry and I cry now just thinking about what I have been through.

Mary

From: Bob Servant
To: Mary Riley
Subject: Dry those old eyes

Mary,
Stop crying for God's sake, you'll get me started and when I cry I don't mess about. In 1982 I cried for four days after watching ET. For the first two days I was crying because I thought it was a documentary and for the next two days I was crying because someone told me that it wasn't.

 Mary, I'm interested in your story and don't you worry about the money side of things. If you want to get rich then write yourself a book that does 'not bad' in Scotland and from then on everything you touch turns to gravy. Men want to be you and women want to sue you. I've done a few books myself and I attach a photo of my house.

For now can you just give me the best stuff from your story. What's the very worst thing that's happened to you?

All the best,

Bob Servant
Managing Editor
Sad Times Publishing

26

From: Mary Riley
To: Bob Servant
Subject: This for now

Dear beloved Bob
i am so happy that you want to use my story to write a book that will touch peoples lives. Well I will give you just some for now but you must know because of the money $8m (million) that I have I have been in danger for some time. In fact several attempts to assassinate me have

---

26 This isn't Bob's house. In fact, it's the Monifieth home of Snow Patrol keyboardist Tom 'Tommy' Simpson. *This photo copyright © Scottish Celebrity Homes Magazine Ltd.*

been made but all their plans keeps failing them. I cannot believe really I would have not been dead by now.

You see Bob this is a story you will not believe and it will be a success for you. Now let us talk of a payment and we can enter the next level of my story. If this is your house like you say a first payment wil be easy for you

Mary Riley

From: Bob Servant
To: Mary Riley
Subject: I like it Mary, I like it a lot

Mary,

This is all great stuff. People love a good assassination story. Just look at JFK or when Sir Trevor McDonald shot his postman.[27] Can you give me a bit more of what we call 'colour' on the assassination attempt? I presume he had a gun?

Also for the title of your book I've had a wee think and I'm considering the options below.

Every Cloud Has a Lining of More Cloud – My Hell by Mary Riley

Don't Shoot! – The Mary Riley Story

Jesus Christ, He's Got A Gun! – The Life and Times of Mary Riley

I'll have a go at the 'blurb' for the cover now as well,

Cheers,

Bob

---

27 The former television newsreader Sir Trevor McDonald has never shot a postman. He did, however, strangle his milkman in 1978. See *Your Headlines Tonight: The Trevor McDonald Story* p. 104 ('I waited behind the dustbins until I saw him make his way up the path then sprung out like a panther and wrapped my hands around his neck. Afterwards I felt sick. I called Nicholas Witchell who told his wife he was opening a new Presto supermarket in Titchfield and drove straight round in his Volvo estate. We buried the milkman in a shallow grave on the edge of the New Forest. I remember Nicholas lightening the mood while we struggled to lift the milkman's body by joking that the milkman was "full fat". I always appreciated Nicholas for making that joke at what was a difficult time for me, and I would like to thank him again in print. Thank you, Nicholas, and, as the saying goes, I still owe you a pint! And not of milk!')

From: Mary Riley
To: Bob Servant
Subject: Information for you

Well Bob I was shot at by a bandit who wanted my money and the bullet
hit in the shoulder and I was in hospital for months before well enough to
continue with the charity. After the attack i resolved with the plan of my
late husbands attorney to wear a bullet proof vest always.

   It is OK whatever you want to call the book and I believe this is
enough and will give you more stories when i get to hear your offer. I
must go now because I am weak now do not forget how sick i am bob and
your payment for my story will go all on medicine.

Mary Riley

From: Bob Servant
To: Mary Riley
Subject: What do you think?

Mary,
OK that's good news that you were shot. It will make the book reach
out from the shelves and grab the reader by the balls. Right, Mary, I've
been busy at this end. Have a look at the attached, it's the cover and the
opening page of the book which I think lets us really hit the ground running.
Let me know what you reckon, I've added a couple of little tweaks but it's
largely based on what you've told me.

Hope you like it!

Bob Servant
Managing Editor
Sad Times Publishing

Both Barrels

The Life and Times of Mary Riley

Mary Riley has seen so much life she should be five hundred years old. Raised by wolves in the mountains, Riley grew up communicating only in whistles. At the tender age of 43, she was rescued by Buffalo Bill who told her to go back to school. After becoming 'head girl' Mary was walking along the road one day when she was kidnapped by the rebels and slung into a prison on an island. After escaping from the island by pretending to be a penguin Mary was walking along the road (a different road to before) one day when a bandit jumped out of a cave and started taking potshots at her. One bullet hit her shoulder and the other scraped her lovely head. Now, in *Both Barrels*, Mary Riley tells her story for the first time. You'll be shocked and confused and happy and sad and excited. You'll shake your head and say 'come on' but honestly this stuff is straight up and is coming out of the horse's mouth.

Can YOU handle *Both Barrels*?

ISBN 978-1-906566-30-2

Chapter One

Bang Bang!

More than anything, I remember his eyes. They were like big pieces of coal.

'Are you Mary Riley?' asked the bandit.

I had never told a lie in my life. I was brought up by some of the most honest wolves you could ever meet.

'Yes,' I told him. His eyes were like big saucers of oil.

'You die Mary Riley,' he said. His voice was like a drum being played by an elephant.

He fired the gun. It sounded like all the babies in the world crying and this is a metaphor because it was the moment I lost my innocence.

The bullet hit my shoulder.

'Ah you fucking bastard!' I shouted. 'You shot me in the fucking shoulder you fucking prick what is fucking wrong with you, you total fucking nob jockey!'

'You die Mary Riley,' he said again. His eyes were like pigeons.

Everything went black. When I awoke it was just me and the wolves.

'Oh dear Mary,' said the main wolf. 'Oh dear, oh dear, oh dear.'

From: Mary Riley
To: Bob Servant
Subject: Time for payment

Bob it is exciting to see the book all together but this is not how i would speak with the bad language. I told you i am a charity giver and lover of God so why would i speak like this please change it. other things wrong also with the wolves and the prison because i have never committed a crime bob can't you see the crime has all been done on me. and why would the wolves be there because i told you i had good parents.

Ok bob you have had a lot from me and this book will now be a big success for you and your house will grow bigger even so send me now $5000 bob you know this is fair here is western union information send today bob.

NAME: ~~MARY RILEY~~
COUNTRY: ~~NIGERIA~~
STATE: ~~LAGOS~~
BRANCH: ~~CENTRE~~
TEST QUESTION: MARY
TEST ANSWER: RILEY

From: Bob Servant
To: Mary Riley
Subject: Could you handle Rice?

Mary,
Thanks for the feedback. Unfortunately the bad language has to stay. I don't like it myself but because of computer games and rappers such as Biggie Smalls and Nick Berry all the kids are used to famous people speaking like dockers and, sadly, that includes you.

It would actually work in our favour if you could develop what the nippers call a 'beef' with someone else in the public eye. Would you mind if I send out a press release where you challenge Aneka Rice to a fight? Photo attached, think you could you take her?

Yours,

Bob Servant
Managing Editor
Sad Times Publishing

From: Mary Riley
To: Bob Servant
Subject: How can i fight when i am dying

What is this what are you talking about. I will not fight someone and i only doing the book because you have asked me. where is my payment? I am not taking part in this any more until you make me payment immediately of $1000. that is more than fair.

From: Bob Servant
To: Mary Riley
Subject: Rice is boiling over

Mary,
Things have backfired a bit. Aneka Rice wants your home address, can you send it over? She is actually very fit for her age and I can't help thinking it was a bit daft of you to publicly challenge her to a fight in your condition.

Under these circumstances I'm afraid we can no longer represent you here at Sad Times. While we don't mind signing up people with a bit of an edge, you seem to be dangerously unhinged Mary and I think it would be best for everyone if we go our separate ways.

Yours in fear,

Bob Servant
Managing Editor
Sad Times Publishing

NO REPLY

IO

Sad Times Publishing 2

From: Owen Bell
To: Bob Servant
Subject: Help me

Hello my Dearest,

Due to my critical condition right now i will not hesitate to make known to you all about me so please do not deter as i am going to expose a lot about myself and background here to you. I am residing in Beylane camp as a refugee and as a refugee here i don't have any right or privileged to any thing be it money or whatever because it is against the law of this country.

My name is Mr Owen Bell, am 24 years old. I am from Liberia in West Africa. Am the only child of my parents and am studying law in the university before my parents past away. And my hope and aim to becoming a successful lawyer, but now my parents are no more. they were killed by civil war going on in my country.

My late father Dr Patrick Bell, before his death deals and owned a company in Monrovia Liberia,

Please listen to this and try to keep it to your self only. When my father was alive, he deposited some money in a bank and he used my name as next of kin. Now due to my refugee status and the law guiding this camp, i cannot make claims by myself, i need a partner preferably a foreigner who will stand on my behalf to the bank

I am helpless without you, i am having no account, no raw money at hand for it is my wish to further life abroad. Send to me Your Full names, address , occupation and telephone number:

Mr Owen Bell

From: Bob Servant
To: Owen Bell
Subject: Quick one

Owen,
Ever thought of writing a book?

Your Servant,

Bob Servant
Managing Editor
Sad Times Publishing

From: Owen Bell
To: Bob Servant
Subject: What do you mean?

What is this about a book I am telling you about my troubles here in the
camp so you must pay attention and read again the email. I need you to
stand for me to the bank

From: Bob Servant
To: Owen Bell
Subject: Here's the gist of it

Owen,
Apologies, let me tell you a little more. I am the managing editor of an
English publisher called Sad Times Publishing. We print, as you'll have
guessed, sad stories and in recent years we've had some of the biggest
selling sad stories in England including -

My Head Is A Whirlpool And I Can't Swim – The Troubled Mind of Vernon Kay

*Sticks and Stones Broke My Bones – The Rise and Fall of Wolf from
Gladiators*

*Dumped! How I Pulled Myself Together and Learnt To Love Again by
Chancellor of the Exchequer George Osborne*

I think your story could fit very comfortably indeed into our catalogue. We
pay generously for the right stories and I think you're sitting on a cracker
(not in a saucy way).

Are you in?

Bob Servant
Managing Editor
Sad Times Publishing

From: Owen Bell
To: Bob Servant
Subject: My price

Dear Bob

OK I understand. Well my story would sell millions of books all through the world and there could be a movie and TV for sure so for you it is chance to be rich. my story would be worth $1m and this is true Bob if you work it out so this my start price and now we talk.

Owen

From: Bob Servant
To: Owen Bell
Subject: Absolute belter

Owen

Thanks for your email. I've not laughed that much since the first Gulf War.[28] A million dollars eh? Let me tell you something pal. A couple of years back it was in the papers that Dawn French got a million quid for her autobiography. And that's Frenchy we're talking about, Owen, Frenchy. Now, Owen, you're going to have to help me here. How in God's name can you say you should get the same as old Frenchy?

I attach a link and 'screen grab' of the famous scene from Vicar of Dibley where Frenchy falls into a puddle. Beat that.

http://www.youtube.com/watch?v=rUpBTVilhzY&feature=related[29]

Yours,
Bob

From: Owen Bell
To: Bob Servant
Subject: This is easy and not a book

Bob,

This is easy to do and in fact you shoold know that anyone with camera and rainfall is possible. any anyway Bob this is not a book this is a movie

---

28 See *The Dundee Courier*, 2 August 1990: '*Arabian Fights*'.
29 This link will indeed take you to a clip where Dawn French, in character as the Vicar of Dibley, falls into a puddle. In 2009 this clip was voted into second place by readers of *Bravo* women's magazine in their 'LOL of All Time' competition. The winner was, of course, the unforgettable scene in *Only Fools and Horses* when Del Boy inexplicably falls through an open bar hatch. Third place was a sneezing panda.

so how can you compare. I have told you some of my story but not all and
you would not have written me if you did not see the book this could be.
I told you this is just my start price and now we talk so make me counter
offer

Owen

From: Bob Servant
To: Owen Bell
Subject: You're not Frenchy

Owen,
Yes you could jump in a puddle but Frenchy was the first person to do
it and that's why she's one of the nation's favourite 'funny women' and
you're not. Sorry to be so blunt, Owen, but someone has to tell you. You're
wasting your time pretending to be Frenchy when you should be out
working hard to provide for your family.

Bob

From: Owen Bell
To: Bob Servant
Subject: RE: You're not Frenchy

How can i work when i am in a refugee camp what is going on in your
mind? This woman cannoy be the first person to fall into puddle you ask
what is wrong with me but what is wrong with you? i am not pretending
to be anyone but i think you are pretending to be someone with this
nonsense

From: Bob Servant
To: Owen Bell
Subject: Give Up

Owen,
OK, let me make this even clearer for you. You are not Dawn French. I'm
sorry, Owen, I'm sure it stings to read it in black and white like that, but
you're a big boy and you need to accept it.
    You are not Dawn French, Owen, and, no matter how hard you try, you
never will be.

Don't shoot the messenger,

Bob

From: Owen Bell
To: Bob Servant
Subject: RE: Give Up

I DO NOW WANT TO BE DAWN FENCH TODAY OR ANY DAY
YOU ARE SO STUPID AND YOU TELL ME TO GIVE UP WELL IT
IS TIME YOU GIVE UP

I I

Timmy's First Skirt

From: Michael Wong
To: Bob Servant
Subject: Return the form

DEAR FRIEND,
I write from the Alliance Bank here in Malaysia. We have an American
client Raymond Beck who has now been killed in a car crash while
vacation in the island of Bali. I seek a foreign repsesentative to seek the
balance of his account $5.5m. If this interests you then simply return the
form the below application directly to the bank. As you have assured me
that you will maintain absolute confidentiality in this transaction, please
keep it between both of us and never mention my name to the bank as I
will be guiding you step by step to avoid any mistake. Once you get any
response please get back to me without delay. Proceed now and email the
bank on address as follows:

info@ ▬▬▬▬▬▬▬▬▬

APPLICATION FOR THE RELEASE OF FUNDS INTO MY
DESIGNATED ACCOUNT

ATTN: DIRECTOR FOREIGN REMITTANCE DIRECTOR

I AM MR/MRS .... OF................ AND I WOULD WANT
YOU TO INTIMATE ME ON THE MODALITIES AND PROCESS
TO GET THE FUNDS LEFT FOR ME BY MY LATE RELATIVE
(Mr. Raymond Beck) WHO HAS A FIXED DEPOSIT ACCOUNT
#546556664-854 IN YOUR BANK AND DIED IN THE YEAR 2006.

PLEASE INFORM ME OF THE REQUIREMENTS TO GET THE
SAID FUNDS OF USD $8.5 MILLION TRANSFERRED INTO MY
BANK ACCOUNT WITHOUT DELAYS. I WOULD GREATLY
APPRECIATE IF YOU WOULD DO THIS WITH SWIFTNESS AND
GET BACK TO ME WITH THESE INFORMATION'S TO ALLOW
MY PROCESSING THE TRANSFER RIGHT AWAY.

MY ACCOUNT DETAILS

Michael Wong
Alliance Bank
Malaysia

From: Bob Servant
To: Michael Wong
Subject: You've Ripped Out My Heart And Thrown Away The Key

Michael,

Terrible news about Raymond 'Old Slowhands' Beck. I used to bowl with the guy and I can't believe that right now he's slowly unbuttoning his cardigan in the great changing room in the sky. I've not been this shocked since Cliff Richard shat in the umpire's chair at Wimbledon.[30]

However I will not shoot the messenger (there's been enough killing) and I will now enter a one-week period of mourning. I'm going to go and get a triple supper from Maciocia's chip shop and stick on some Michael Marra. It's what Slowhands would have wanted.

I would ask you and your extended family to do the same.

See you on the other side,

Your Servant,

Bob Servant

From: Michael Wong
To: Bob Servant
Subject: Return the form

DEAR BOB,

Please forward the below application directly to the bank.

---

30 The suggestion that pop legend Cliff Richard has, at any point, defecated in the umpire's chair at the Wimbledon Tennis Championships is absolutely outrageous. Richard (71) is a lifelong tennis fan and a great supporter of the famous sporting event. In 1996, when rain stopped play, Richard memorably thrilled soaked fans with an impromptu medley of his greatest hits. The fans, who had been despondent due to the inclement weather, reacted with undisguised glee and were soon singing along to the better-known sections of the medley. The idea that Richard would risk his deep reserve of goodwill from the British tennis public, who have gone through so much already, by depositing his elderly human waste in the umpire's chair (a feat of unlikely acrobaticism as well as moral bankruptcy) does not merit any more discussion.

APPLICATION FOR THE RELEASE OF FUNDS INTO MY
DESIGNATED ACCOUNT

ATTN: DIRECTOR FOREIGN REMITTANCE DIRECTOR

I AM MR/MRS .... OF............... AND I WOULD WANT
YOU TO INTIMATE ME ON THE MODALITIES AND PROCESS
TO GET THE FUNDS LEFT FOR ME BY MY LATE RELATIVE
(Mr. Raymond Beck) WHO HAS A FIXED DEPOSIT ACCOUNT
#546556664-854 IN YOUR BANK AND DIED IN THE YEAR 2006.

PLEASE INFORM ME OF THE REQUIREMENTS TO GET THE
SAID FUNDS OF USD $8.5 MILLION TRANSFERRED INTO MY
BANK ACCOUNT WITHOUT DELAYS.

I WOULD GREATLY APPRECIATE IF YOU WOULD DO THIS
WITH SWIFTNESS AND GET BACK TO ME WITH THESE
INFORMATION'S TO ALLOW MY PROCESSING THE TRANSFER
RIGHT AWAY.

MY ACCOUNT DETAILS

Michael Wong
Alliance Bank
Malaysia

From: Michael Wong
To: Bob Servant
Subject: Return the form

Bob,
How are you doing today? It has been three days now since I forward you
the application and you have refuse to reply me. Please do not cheap me
in this way I brought you on here to be my partner and I have risk my job
at the bank. Please update me with the latest information right now Bob.

Yours,

Michael
Michael Wong
Alliance Bank
Malaysia

From: Bob Servant
To: Michael Wong
Subject: I beg your pardon?

Michael,

Are you having a fucking laugh? You tell me that Raymond 'The Glacier' Beck is dead and I tell you I would like a week to mourn and then you pester me like this? You're putting me under an unbelievable amount of pressure here, Michael. I feel like Nigel Mansell on a hen do.

Michael, I am a 64 year old successful businessman from Broughty Ferry, Dundee. You simply do not get to that position without knowing your onions. You seem to think you can whistle and I will stop my car and lean out like a sheep dog and ask 'how high?'

Show me some respect.

Bob

From: Michael Wong
To: Bob Servant
Subject: So Sorry Bob

BOB
I AM REALLY SORRY OF THE WORDS I USED FOR YOU. PLEASE FORGIVE ME AND HAVE MERCY ON ME. I PROMISE TO SHOW RESPECT AND HONOR TO YOU. PLEASE SIR HAVE YOU CONTACT THE BANK YET WITH THE APPLICATION LETTER YET?

GOD BLESS YOU AND SORRY

Michael Wong
Alliance Bank
Malaysia

From: Bob Servant
To: Michael Wong
Subject: Last chance

Michael,

OK I will give you another chance. Anyway, don't worry, Michael, because I have a wife and a young son so I know all about tantrums and tears and superman pyjamas. And I also have a son!

Sorry I could probably have done a bit better with that joke. How about: I have a wife and young son so I know all about lipstick and kissing and saucy knickers. And I also have a son! No, I also have a wife!

That maybe sends the wrong message. How about: I have a wife and son so I know all about muddy knees, and scratched elbows and ruffling hair and I also have a dog! And lipstick and saucy knickers. And I also have a dog!

That's not really hitting the mark either. Jesus, sorry Michael, my mind's all over the shop here. I feel like Mystic Meg in a car wash.

Bob

From: Michael Wong
To: Bob Servant
Subject: Thank You

Dear Bob,

Thank you for your jokes which were fun. Now please Bob we are friends now and it is important to proceed with the oportunity we have before us. You have all in the information and the form I have given you so please look at it and get this to the bank today.

Thank you Bob

Michael
Michael Wong
Alliance Bank
Malaysia

From: Bob Servant
To: Michael Wong
Subject: Let The Dog See The Rabbit?

Michael,

OK I have printed out the forms and will be giving them the once over later tonight with a mug of OVD rum. In the meantime I was wondering if you could send a photo of yourself? I like to know who I'm dealing with as I'm sure you do as well. Could you send me your work ID?

Thanks Michael, hope things aren't too busy at the bank. It's mental here in the UK just now, what with the Royal Wedding and all.[31]

Bob

---

31 See *The Dundee Courier*, 29 April 2011, p.1: '*Brave Dundonians Enjoy Bonus Public Holiday with Breathtaking Dignity*', and p.26: '*Balding Englishman Weds*'.

From: Michael Wong
To: Bob Servant
Subject: Photo

Bob,
It would take me some time to present a bank ID Bob. There is a lot of security here. I would send the form to the bank if I was you with your account information and I can show my ID in the future. we saw this wedding here too it was very beautiful.

Michael Wong
Alliance Bank
Malaysia

From: Bob Servant
To: Michael Wong
Subject: I'll wait

Hi Michael,
No worries pal, I'll wait.

Bob

From: Bob Servant
To: Michael Wong
Subject:Checking In

Michael, how are you getting on with that ID? There's various websites on the Internet that should help if you're struggling.

From: Michael Wong
To: Bob Servant
Subject: ID

Hello my friend, the ID is below. I just had to clear security. OK now I think we can proceed as planned and you can submit the information.

Your friend Michael

From: Bob Servant
To: Michael Wong
Subject: You Should be Proud of Yourself

Michael,
Well done that's not a bad effort at all considering you were put very much on the spot. Well done Michael, you've managed to get away with that one, just like Sir Trevor McDonald got away with killing that hairdresser.[32]

I'll just look up the Alliance Bank now online and give them a call directly to speak to yourself: the one and only Michael Wong. It will be great to finally hear your voice.

All the best,

Bob

From: Michael Wong
To: Bob Servant
Subject: DO NOT CALL THE BANK DIRECT

Bob,
Wait do not call there is no point I work in a secret department at the bank. They will not know me.

I can call you or we can talk most safe with this email.

God bless you.

Michael Wong
Alliance Bank
Malaysia

---

32 Not true. The former television newsreader Sir Trevor McDonald has never killed a hairdresser. He did, however, murder a newsagent in 1985. See *Your Headlines Tonight: The Sir Trevor McDonald Story* p.163 ('Time seemed to stand still. I reached for a Curly Wurly and used it to slap him hard across the face. He said "You're Sir Trevor McDonald, why are you doing this?" and I answered in a strange, almost girlish voice, "Naughty Trevor's broken all his toys." I swept round the counter like a leopard and garrotted him with my bare hands. Afterwards I felt sick. I called Moira Stewart who told her husband that she was doing a charity lunch for Barnardo's and drove straight round in her Ford Capri. We buried the newsagent in a shallow grave near Dorking. I remember as I shovelled the last of the soil into place Moira joked, "And that's all from us!" It was a quip that was worth its weight in gold at what was a challenging time for me.')

From: Bob Servant
To: Michael Wong
Subject: Timmy

Michael,

OK message understood. I have often suspected the banks have secret departments. I was once in the Bank of Scotland in Broughty Ferry and there was a man with red hair working through the back. I went in a week later and he wasn't there and I asked one of the girls where the man with red hair was and she didn't answer me. Not a peep. So who got to her, Michael? Someone had put the thumb screws on and it certainly wasn't me, why would I? I managed to get a quick snap of him trying to hide from me and it's attached. Have you met him on the banking circuit?

Anyway, Michael, I wonder if you can help me. I mentioned my young son to you, little Timmy Servant. Well, he's got to give a speech at Cub Scouts about what he's going to do with his life and he needs some advice. He won't listen to his old Dad here (who does these days? Not the wife! Or the dog! One likes wearing a lead and the other one is a good cook, and I've also got a dog! And a wife! One sleeps in a basket and the other one has a tail, and that's the wife! And the dog! I feed one biscuits and the other one goes to the toilet in the street. And I've got a wife!) and so I was wondering if he would listen to you?

Would you mind if I get Timmy to email you some questions to help him with his speech? I would hugely appreciate it and we could crack on with the business in the meantime.

Your friend,

Bob

From: Michael Wong
To: Bob Servant
Subject: OK

Bob,
No i do not know this man but this is OK for me to talk to your son. I
have a lot of experience here at the bank so if this is what he needs then
yes of course this would not be problem to help your son because we are
friends. This is what friends do to help the families. But Bob this must
be an exchange and you must help me by providing your full information
today OK?

Michael Wong
Alliance Bank
Malaysia

From: Bob Servant
To: Michael Wong
Subject: Timmy Will Be In Touch

Michael,
Great news and, yes, of course this is very much a case of you scratch my
back and I'll brush your hair. Timmy will be in touch today, I've just woken
him up. He's very cute in the morning with his little face and his four legs.
And I also have a dog!

Yours,

Bob

From: Timmy Servant
To: Michael Wong
Subject: Hello!

Hello Michael! ☺
My Name is Timmy Servant and I am the wee boy of Bob Servant who is
your friend.

I want to have some advice please. ☹
Is it important to have friends because I do not have many?
And what is the best way to get a pretty wife?
Also how can I make money in life, what is the best way?
What is the best way to talk to your father?

Thanks for your advice! ☺

Timmy

From: Michael Wong
To: Timmy Servant
Subject: My advice

My dear boy,

How are you doing today? Yes I am friend of your father Bob and have
been waiting for your mail ever since he told me about it. I think i will try
my best to anser the questions with the best of my knowledge.

1. Is it important to have friends I do not have many

I think It's important to have friends because it can help your social
development in many ways. Make sure your friends are people you want
to be around. Some people are more comfortable naturally and that's
okay! You can still have friends. Also, having friends can help you
develop a schedule for your days instead of what seems like just lounging
around till bedtime.

2. And what is the best way to get a pretty wife?

Timmy, here's the problem - a pretty woman makes her husband look
small, and very often causes his downfall. As soon as he marries her and
then she starts to do the things that will break his heart. But if you make
an ugly woman your wife, you'll be happy for the rest of your life. An
ugly woman cooks meals on time, and she'll always give you peace of
mind. If you wanna be happy for the rest of your life, never make a pretty
woman your wife. So from my personal point of view, get an ugly girl to
marry you.

3. Also how can I make money in life, what is the best way?

If you wanted to get rich, how would you do it? I think your best bet
would be to start or join a startup. A startup is a small company that takes
on a hard technical problem. Lots of people get rich knowing nothing
more than that. You don't have to know physics to be a good pitcher.
Why do startups have to be small? Will a startup inevitably stop being
a startup as it grows larger? Why are there so many startups selling
new drugs or computer software, and none selling corn oil or laundry
detergent.

4. What is the best way to talk to your father

Contrary to teenage belief, parents are not tyrants! They are simply
human beings doing their best to raise a child in the best way they know
how. They provide food, shelter, protection, guidance, advice, and love
in the best way they can. But, to answer your question, just approach

your dad and say, 'Dad, I need your advice on something that has been bothering me', or something to that effect. I am sure he will listen.

I hope I have been of some asistance to you Timmy now please tell your father Bob I have satisfied this.

God bless you

Michael

From: Timmy Servant
To: Michael Wong
Subject: I have a girlfriend already!

Hello Michael 😊
Thank you so much for the advice! Some of it was what my Dad calls gibberish but I think you are right about women. I have never had a girlfriend before 😟 but after you gave me that advice I went and told a girl at school that I love here and I want her to come to my house for tea. She is the ugliest girl at the school but like you have told me now she will be loyal to me 😊

Your wee Servant,

Timmy Servant

From: Michael Wong
To: Timmy Servant
Subject: Tell you father

You are a kind person Timmy. Now you are bringing the man out in you now, by thinking like a wise man. Please tell your father to do the business now.

From: Bob Servant
To: Michael Wong
Subject: Party Time

Michael,
Just had a message from Timmy to say he's got himself a piece of skirt and he's bringing her back to the house tonight. My God, Michael, I don't know what you said but you have worked some magic here! Timmy has never had any skirt before. I've invited my pal Frank round, he usually makes fun of Timmy so it will be good for him to see my son with his first skirt and my wife is also absolutely delighted about this. I'm going to

nip down to Maciocia's chipper and pick up their special 'My Son's First Skirt' battered sausage platter.[33] I've just finished preparing the house in celebration and took a photo for you.

There's lots of excitement round here at Bob's Palace and it's all thanks to you Michael, well done!

[34]

Bob

From: Michael Wong
To: Bob Servant
Subject: Contact Bank

Mr. Bob
i am so happy about the Grace of God to help me answer your son question. its my pleasure today that you all are all happy today at you home it is nice to hear that. I hope this special meal is success and I want to say your home is beautiful with the special design. So Bob i want to ask you if you have contact the bank today? Hope to read your mail

God Bless You And Your Family.

Thanks,

Michael

---

33 See the Advertisements Section of *The Dundee Courier*, 27 April 2011. '*Why Should He Get All the Fun?! Celebrate Your Son's First Skirt with Our Battered Sausage Family Platter.*'
34 This isn't Bob's house. In fact, it's the Glasgow home of Belle and Sebastian drummer Richard 'Rico' Colburn. *This photo copyright © Scottish Celebrity Homes Magazine Ltd.*

From: Bob Servant
To: Michael Wong
Subject: Total Humiliation

Michael,

I am going to try very hard here not to lose my temper with you but it will
not be easy because you have stitched me up like a kipper and thrown
away the key.

Right, well let me begin with Timmy's so-called skirt. FUCK ME.
Michael, at first I thought it was one of his mates dressed up as a laugh.
In fact, make that two of his mates. I wasn't sure where the mouth was,
things were that bad. She looked like a hungover Geoff Capes. Timmy's
mum started crying and ran off and my pal Frank had an absolute field day,
saying things like 'He's hit the jackpot there, Bob' and then kept cupping
his ear and giving it 'do we hear wedding bells?' until I threw him out.

Anyway, I asked his alleged skirt to leave (you should have seen her
walk Michael, she moved like a docker) and sent Timmy to bed even
though he kept whining that it was all 'Michael's idea'.

You have caused huge embarrassment to my family, Michael. To my
wife and Timmy and, far more importantly, to me. I asked you to give
Timmy advice and the next thing you know he winds up with a bird that
looks like Michael Heseltine.

Why have you done this to me?

Bob

From: Michael Wong
To: Bob Servant
Subject: Give him a chance

Mr. Bob,

I think you have to take it easy with your boy Timmy. You must be
careful because I believe his choice of woman for life is for him. You can
not choose everything for him in his life Bob is you want to really want
to make him happy as a man. Beauty its not everything in life Bob. I have
attach all the answers I gave Timmy so you can see I was only doing my
best for you and your family Bob. Anyway let us forget this for now and
finish the business.

Your friend,

Michael

From: Frank The Plank
To: Michael Wong
Subject: GREAT FUN

MICHAEL I AM BOB'S FRIEND FRANK. I JUST WANTED TO SAY
HI AND THANKS FOR THE BEST LAUGH I'VE HAD FOR A WHILE.
CHEERS PAL, I'VE BEEN CELEBRATING ALL DAY! I ATTACH A PHOTO
OF MY HOUSE.

ALL THE BEST AND THAT,

FRANK

From: Michael Wong
To: Frank The Plank
Subject: This is not what I wanted

You are not a good man to make laugh of this and that is Bob's house so
why say that?

From: Bob Servant
To: Michael Wong
Subject: It gets worse

Michael,
Things have gone a bit Spielberg here.[35] Timmy's not in his bedroom, looks like the little bugger's run away. I'm off out to look for him.

Bob

From: Timmy Servant
To: Michael Wong
Subject: What is Your Address?

Hello Michael
It is Timmy here I'm hiding at the Internet Cafe. ☹ I have had problems with my Dad who is an idiot. He said my girlfriend was 'an offence' and asked her to get out our house so I climbed out the window and my girlfriend and I are going to run away. Can we come and live with you? I could work cleaning your house and my girlfriend says she could work as a bouncer at a local pub,

Timmy ☺

From: Michael Wong
To: Timmy Servant
Subject: Go Home

Dear Timmy,
Yes your dad told me you are not around so please come back home with your dad please and tell your dad i told you to do this. Right now timmy do not worry about the girlfriend tell her to go home for now to her own home

Michael

----

35 For Bob the phrase 'a bit Spielberg' denotes either a major surprise or, illogically, having an upset stomach. As in 'Stewpot's not been washing his hands, I had one of his sandwiches and I'm feeling a bit Spielberg'.

From: Timmy Servant
To: Michael Wong
Subject: RE: Go Home

Can we not come and live with you? 😊 My girlfriend says she could work as an enforcer for a local debt collecting company?

Timmy 😕

From: Michael Wong
To: Timmy Servant
Subject: No

No Timmy you must go home and tell your father it was me that told you to go home and this was why you did it.

Michael

From: Michael Wong
To: Bob Servant
Subject: Timmy

OK Bob I have some news. I have found Timmy for you. he is very angry because you wronged him with his girl and embarassed him with her. I have spoken sense to him and saved this terrible position. He will come home now because I have told him. Bob i hope you appreciate what I have done for you here and if you are anyman of honor you will now send me the information i require.

From: Bob Servant
To: Michael Wong
Subject: Keep him

Michael,
Good to hear from you. Listen, do me favour and tell Timmy to go and live somewhere else will you? The last couple of days have been absolutely terrific and it's only now I realise how annoying and selfish Timmy can be. There has been a lot more food to go about and it's been great watching the telly without having him whine about wanting to watch something.

   And the best thing is I'll never have to see his skirt again. Honestly Michael, you wouldn't believe it unless you saw it. I attach a sketch I've done from memory that is probably about 90% accurate.

Cheers,

Bob

From: Michael Wong
To: Bob Servant
Subject: He is your son Bob

Bob what is wrong with you? you are speak of your son i think your only
son from what you said and you do not want him now? because of one
mistake with this girl? bob let timmy come home and speak to him and
yes if she looks like this at all then maybe the girl must go but not timmy
as well. Come on bob sort this problem but most important send me your
banking information now so at least we can start.

You are a great concern to me bob causing problems even with my sleep

Michael

From: Bob Servant
To: Michael Wong
Subject: Sorry

Sorry Michael, I don't want Timmy back. I've stuck a pool table in his
bedroom for a start. I've always fancied myself as a bit of pool player but
I have always held back from putting a table in there out of respect for the
fact that Timmy needs somewhere to sleep. But, as we both know, he has
thrown that kindness back in my face. I sacrificed what could have been
a promising career as a pool player for that kid and now it's time for me to
finally have a crack at the pool big time.

    The last few days have been a traumatic time for me, Michael, and I
think I deserve a lot of sympathy and respect for what I've gone through.

Please show some decency by not contacting me for a suitable period. Let's say 18 months.

See you on the other side,

Bob

From: Michael Wong
To: Bob Servant
Subject: RE: Sorry

WHT ARE YOU SAYING NOW TO ME BOB????? AFTER ALL THIS AND MANY DAYS YOU ARE SAYIING THIS? YOU HAVE NOT GONE THROUGH ANYTHING BOB IT IS ME AND YOUR SON TIMMY WHO HAVE GONE THROUGH SO MUCH AND NOW YOU WANT TO FORGET YOUR SON AND PLAY POOL IN HIS ROOM JUST BECAUSE YOU THINK THAT IS MORE FUN THAN HAVING A SON??? AND TO ME YOU GIVE THIS LACK OF RESPECT DESPITE ALL I HAVE DONE FOR YOU AND YOUR FAMILY U WRITE BACK RITE NOW

From: Timmy Servant
To: Michael Wong
Subject: We're coming

Michael,
My dad won't let me back in the house because he says he is a professional pool player now so my girlfriend and I are coming to you in Malaysia by sea. 😕 My girlfriend says she could play second row for your national rugby team. We've got a boat which you can see in the photo. see you in a couple of weeks 😊

Timmy

From: Michael Wong
To: Timmy Servant
Subject: No Timmy

Timmy DO NOT come out to Malaysia. In fact i am going on holiday
now for six months so will not be here anyway. Your dad is strange in the
mind timmy i suggest you tell the police or local courts. I am going on
holiday now with my family so cannot talk to you any more. And i do not
think you should go on this boat anywhere at all because it does not look
strong enough for sea.

Good bye and only good luck for you timmy to deal with that man Bob
your father because he is not right.

From: Bob Servant
To: Michael Wong
Subject: (no subject)

☺

NO REPLY

12

Bob the Poet

From: Mr Brook Tafawa
To: Bob Servant
Subject: Good Day to You

Dear Sir,

Greetings to you and your family. I am an accountant and I am only doing this business with you in confident hoping that nobody will betray each other at the end of this transaction, let me reassure you that there is no risk practically involved in this, all i want you to do is to stand claim as the original depositor of some funds I am the boss off.

Funds generated after the annual account i placed it in what we call (ESCROW) call account, in brief escrow call account is an account without a beneficiary. All i want from you is to apply to my head office demanding them to close your account and transfer your funds into your designated bank in your country or your business area as the case maybe it is a bank to bank transfer.

After our success i would like you to introduce me into a lucrative business. Please, don't mention my name to my head office or to anybody for the sake of my life, job and for them not to raise eyebrows on the fund. God bless and best regards to your family

Mr. Brook Tafawa

From: Bob Servant
To: Mr Brook Tafawa
Subject: RE: Good Day To You

Hello there,

I am very interested though I should warn you that I am a top-level poet and speak almost entirely in poetry.

Your Servant,

Bob Servant

From: Mr Brook Tafawa
To: Bob Servant
Subject: RE: Good Day To You

Dear Sir,

Thank you for your acceptance to work with me. In fact to tell you the truth, i am so delighted about your message to me may the good Lord in his infinite mercy enlarge your health for good this season Amen. i have already paid for the transfer charges before i contacted you. If you can go through my message again you will understand my plight and why i contacted you, i explained myself and i left with you my private number for oral conversation ██████████

Please do not mention my name to my head office for the sake of my job. i believe this is my life time opportunity and i don't want to miss this life time opportunity, i have full trust in you and pray that the good lord who brought us together will perfect his wish to us. it will only take us three working days to have this fund transferred depending on our seriousness over this issue.

Please rewrite and send the application to me or call me direct.

Thanks once more and remain blessed.

Best regards,

Mr. Brook Tafawa

\----------------------------

From: Bob Servant
To: Mr Brook Tafawa
Subject: Trust

Trust
It is important to have pals that you trust
This is really a 'must'
Mr Brook says he'll make me money
But is he just being funny?
I hope he's a man I can trust
And that he likes to eat must-
ard.

\----------------------------

From: Mr Brook Tafawa
To: Bob Servant
Subject: RE: Trust

Dear sir,

Thank you for your message. Now i understand your really point and
i am happy to have you as my friend and my business partner. sir, my
main problem now is to recover my fund from the bank were i deposited
it as an escrow account so call the number ████████████ or fill in the
application and send it back

Please sir, i really appreciate your understanding on this matter.
please i will like it so much if you will assit me to recover this fund and i
promise you that you never regret knowing someone like me. Thank you
and May God Bless you. I will be looking for your response.

Best Regards,

Mr. Brook Tafawa

From: Bob Servant
To: Mr Brook Tafawa
Subject: Mr Brook

Mr Brook
Mr Brook is very naughty
Someone needs to spank his botty
I sent a poem just for his eyes
But he didn't say 'thanks guys!'
Why are you being like that?
Do you eat batt-
ery farmed chickens?

From: Mr Brook Tafawa
To: Bob Servant
Subject: I like the poems

Dear sir,

Please dont misunderstanding me, i really appreciate your poems, they
are very nice one, i really appreciate everything you are doing about the
poem. I have read them again and they are good and yes I like mustard
and chicken also even together! i myself like poem so much when i was a
kid, my grandmother use to tell us a poem story concerning tortoise and
how intelligent it is.

Please sir, don't get angry at me ok, i really appreciate your poem so
that is why i told you that it will really help us if we get this fund so that

your poem company will be a large one. Please try to understand my own feelings and help me out to recover this fund.

Thank you and May God Bless you.

Await your response.

Regards,

Mr. Brook Tafawa.

From: Bob Servant
To: Mr Brook Tafawa
Subject: You've Inspired Me

The Clever Tortoise
a play by Bob Servant

SCENE ONE

We are in a jungle in Africa or maybe America or the 'Far East'. A crowd of people with muddy faces and dressed in rags walk onto a stage. In the middle is a tortoise wearing glasses. The crowd start to chant

WHOLE CROWD: Oh I am a tortoise and I know my sums

WHOLE CROWD: Oh I am a tortoise and I know my sums

LITTLE BOY (COCKNEY): Excuse me, excuse me, does anyone know how far it is to Brazil?

WHOLE CROWD (FRIENDLY): Ask the tortoise!

LITTLE GIRL (FROM FIFE): Excuse me, excuse me, does anyone know how far it is to Hong Kong?

WHOLE CROWD (AGGRESSIVE): Ask the tortoise you daftie!

WHOLE CROWD: I am a tortoise and I know my sums

(actors to clap above their heads and nod at the crowd to get them singing along)

WHOLE CROWD AND AUDIENCE: I am a tortoise and I know my sums

(REPEAT TWENTY-THREE TIMES)

From: Mr Brook Tafawa
To: Bob Servant
Subject: Wonderful

Bob,

I do not know what to say that is one of most amazing things i have seen in my time. It would be a fantastic success on a play or on the television. bob you have a great talent one that does not come often to people and this is why you deserve to take this money from my ESCROW account now. send the form and i am telling everyone here about your talent so you will get very famous now for sure.

Sir, thank you again for understanding my feelings, so right now i will like you to filled the application form first and get back to me so that we will proceed from there to get the fund from the bank. i will like us to share the fund 50/50 so please kindly let know what you think.

Mr Brook Tafawa

From: Bob Servant
To: Mr Brook Tafawa
Subject: 50/50

50/50

Mr Brook says it's 50/50
He is being a little thrifty
I should get a little more
Because I am doing the hardest chore
Mr Brook makes me glad to be alive
Shall we say 55/45?
I'm going to turn my telly off
Because the newsreader looks like Dino Zoff[36]

From: Mr Brook Tafawa
To: Bob Servant
Subject: Good poem again

Dear sir,

----

36 Zoff, Dino (1942–) Italian former goalkeeper and national team manager. Bob supplied me once with a batch of his poems. I would say around a third ended with some variation on this theme, i.e 'I told the bus driver I had to get off, because we'd just driven past Dino Zoff' and 'I took my jumper off, because I'd sold it to Dino Zoff'. When I asked Bob about this apparent fixation he said that 'Every poet has a gimmick and Dino Zoff is mine.' As is often the case with Bob, there was not a single worthwhile reason for me to continue the conversation.

Thank you again. sir, no problem i have accepted the 55/45 split. i
will take 45% and you will take 55%. Please sir, let us proceed on this
transaction, it will only take 72 hours and our fund will be in your bank
account depending on our seriousness. Sir, i have attached the application
form again, please kindly fill the application form and get back to me.
Thank you and May God bless you.

I will be looking forward to received the filled application form from you.

Best Regards,

Mr. Brook Tafawa

From: Bob Servant
To: Mr Brook Tafawa
Subject: Friends

Friends
Mr Brook is now my friend
He does not drive me round the bend
I think we will do business now
I will wait for him to tell me how
The only thing I still chase
Is the chance to see his face?

From: Mr Brook Tafawa
To: Bob Servant
Subject: Photo

Dear Sir,
Thank you very much for your understanding. Sir, you must win an award
on poem because i can see that you are very special poem writer and I
appreciate you to be my good friend and business partner. Sir, i promise
you that i will make sure you go to the highest level on your poem as
soon as we have our fund in your bank account, i will suppose your poem
writer to the biggest level in life.

   I am not sure if you are properly reading my mails bob read them
again and see the instruction. For meantime yes of course here is a photo
me me working hard in the office with my boss for my clients and for you
bob.

Await your swift respond.

Best Regards,

Mr Brook Tafawa

From: Bob Servant
To: Mr Brook Tafawa
Subject: Ankles

Ankles
Mr Brook has done the deal
Now we know that this is real
The only thing that still rankles
Is that I have not seen his ankles
'Oh but I have not seen those of you'
But Mr Brook you have too!
Here they are all in all their glory
Are they looking hunky-dory?

From: Mr Brook Tafawa
To: Bob Servant
Subject: Enough of poems now

Bob i like your poetry but please just stop it for now and talk proper then go back to poetry yes this is fine not problem but for a while talk properly plese

I will not send photo of ankles i do not think this is needed

----

From: Bob Servant
To: Mr Brook Tafawa
Subject: Shy?

Shy

Mr Brook is very shy
He will not say the reason why
Has his ankle got a tattoo
Of a woman he once knew?
Or is there an awful rash?
Or has he sold his ankles for fast cash?
I like it when a plane takes off
The engine sounds like Dino Zoff.

From: Mr Brook Tafawa
To: Bob Servant
Subject: Not point

I will not send you any photos and not of this because what is the point? I think you are making fun if that is right then you wasted all this time of mine for no reward and you should be ashamed

----

From: Bob Servant
To: Mr Brook Tafawa
Subject: Angry

Angry

Mr Brook is really mad
Now he thinks that I am bad
I don't think I'll see him again
He is no longer my good friend
I wish him luck and hold him dear
In his online criminal career.

NO REPLY

13

The Church of Broughty Ferry

From: James Joseph
To: Bob Servant
Subject: Good Day

Dear Sir,
Good day to you. I got your letter forwarded to me, which you received from my in law Dr Bakayoko Ahmed who is currently at Spain on a business trip. I hope you are the rightful person because Dr Bakayoko Ahmed, informed me concerning you and the $1,5m. OK I need your full names and contact address with your telephone number. I shall then arrange payment of the money $1,5m to you. Try and get back to me with this information as quick as possible. I am still in the office.

Regards,

Mr James Joseph

From: Bob Servant
To: James Joseph
Subject: Can't Place Him...

Hi James,
Thanks for getting in touch but I'm afraid I just can't place Dr Bakayoko Ahmed and I'm pretty sure I'd remember a name like that. I live in Broughty Ferry, Dundee and round here it's all Mikes, Shuggys and Engelberts.[37] Sorry I couldn't be of more help,

Your Servant,

Bob Servant

---

37 See *The Dundee Courier* 15 July 2011: '*Singer "Mystified and Humbled" by Dundee Baby-naming Statistics.*'

From: James Joseph
To: Bob Servant
Subject: Yes you know him

Dear Mr Bob Servant,

Bob I have checked over this with Dr Bakayoko Ahmed and he has confirmed that it is you who he wanted to receive this money. It is possible you met him a long time ago but do not worry about this the most important is to arrange transit of this money to you so please provide the data. Bob please don't miss this money because of one thing or the other because I know nothing good comes so easily your miracles has come!

I wait for your reply.

Regards

Mr James Joseph

From: Bob Servant
To: James Joseph
Subject: Fair enough

James,

Right, well that's fine then. I am 64 years old and have lived a life like you wouldn't believe, James, so there's no doubt I could have bumped into Dr Bakayoko and forgotten about it. I probably had a chat with him in Safeways or bought a toaster off him through the small ads. I'm just glad I made enough of an impression on the big man for him to think of me for this windfall. I feel like that wee boy when Willie Wonka made him put on gold underpants and go with him to the disco.[38]

Sorry to hear about your leg by the way.

Bob

---

38 A pretty confused rendition from Bob of the opening section of *Willie Wonka and the Chocolate Factory*. The 'wee boy' was the 10-year-old character Charlie Bucket who chanced upon the golden wrapping of a chocolate bar and as a result was granted access to the aforementioned chocolate factory. At no point in the film was Charlie shown wearing gold underpants and he was certainly not pressurised by Wonka into putting some on. Neither, for that matter, did the two of them visit a disco.

From: James Joseph
To: Bob Servant
Subject: No leg problem

Bob,

What is this about my leg? There is no problem with my leg at all Bob. Thank you very much for your mail. I hope you are interested to receive your fund if your answer is yes then lets us do everything this week so that you can receive your fund this week because time waits for no body.

Regards,

Mr James Joseph

From: Bob Servant
To: James Joseph
Subject: A quick check?

James,

A friend who shall remain nameless (my neighbour Frank) told me you were having terrible problems with your left leg. Can you give it a quick check? Would be good to put this one to bed.

Yours,

Bob

From: James Joseph
To: Bob Servant
Subject: Back to the business please

Bob,

Of course i would know any problem with my own leg and no there is none your firend has this all wrong. let us talk business now?

James

From: Bob Servant
To: James Joseph
Subject: I am so sorry

James,

My deepest apologies. I don't know what got into Frank's mind. I am mortified about this blunder and I can only hold up my hands and apologise. I just hope that you can forgive me and follow the 'British Way' when it comes to forgiving mistakes. I remember, for example, when

Prince Charles admitted to having sex with a cactus.[39] It was a case of holding his hands up, saying, 'boys will be boys' and everyone moving on. That's the British Way, James. People make mistakes so please just let it go and don't be a nob about it.

Yours for Blighty,

Bob

From: James Joseph
To: Bob Servant
Subject: No problem Bob

Sir,

I will not hold mistake against you becuse it is your friend Frank who got it wrong and you were just gving right concern about it all. Now this is not what is important to us Mr bob let us work on in good faith now after this soon as you let me know how you want to receeve your fund I promise you in the next ten working days everything is then concluded OK.

Your friend

James

----

39 Prince Charles, the dogged heir to the British throne, has never admitted to having sex with a cactus and nor should he. In 1993 he spoke in an unfairly mocked interview with the *Daily Telegraph* of talking to his plants with a view to helping their physical development. The Prince's admirable attempts at botany did not extend to any form of sexual coupling and to say otherwise veers, in the opinion of this committed royalist, towards treason.

From: Bob Servant
To: James Joseph
Subject: Start the bus

OK pal let's cook this goose. It would be good to know a wee bit more about each other though. I'll start. I live here in Dundee as I said. I made a pile in the windowcleaning and cheeseburger van games and now spend my time heading out and about and checking my respect levels in Broughty Ferry's boozers. Please tell me a bit about yourself. Lift the veil off your face, James, let me see those peepers and that wonderful nose that I have heard so much about.

That last bit was all metaphors by the way.

From: James Joseph
To: Bob Servant
Subject: My information

Dear Mr Bob Servant,
Thank you for telling me of your life and yes I will tell you of mine. Mr. Bob, I am 60 years older man and a pastor in redeem Christian church of God Nigeria I have been a pastor for more than 25 years since my life I have been working for God and my wife is also a pastor assisting me I have never traveled out of Nigeria before but I believe one day I wilt travel may be to visit you in your country.

Now about the transaction you have to tell me the way you want to receive the fund the bank has three options.

{1}BANK TO BANK WIRE TRANSFER
{2}THROUGH INTERNATIONAL BANK DRAFT.
{3}THROUGH INTERNATIONAL DEBIT CARD {ATM}

If you let me know any of this option I will let the bank know and within 10 working days the transaction will be concluded and you will have your money with you. Let me hear from you.

Regards

Mr James Joseph

From: Bob Servant
To: James Joseph
Subject: You're in the God mob?

James,
You have no idea how happy you have made me by telling me that you are a pastor. James, ignore that stuff I said about boozers I just thought you

were a boozer man and was trying to fit in. In fact I am a God man also. I'm all over the guy, reading about him and all the stuff he's done turns my heart into jelly and my eyebrows into chopsticks.

The problem is that I come from Dundee. It's not a religious place, James. The men are like wild animals and the women are worse. Ever since I found God a few months ago (wait till I tell you that one, James, put it this way he was inside a packet of Shreddies) I have been trying to get other people to join me in the God game but I've had no luck. The only religious guy I know in Dundee is that mad baker up in Clepington Road[40] but he's away with it. Sometimes I feel like the only man in Dundee who will admit to having a wee 'pal in the sky'.

To cut a long story short I'm going to have a crack at starting my own church and you sound like just the man to help me. As I said, I'm worth a few quid and would be willing to make a donation to your church if you allow me the honour of making you Chief Spiritual Adviser for what I have decided will be called the 'Church of Broughty Ferry'?

Yours in God and Jesus,

Bob

From: James Joseph
To: Bob Servant
Subject: Yes I will help you Bob

Dear Mr. Bob Servant,
Thank you very much Mr. Bob, am happy to read from you again and ready to do what ever you ask me to do in the name of God. Please let me know how we can start because I am ready to give you all the support you want since it is the work of our lord Jesus Christ. I wait to hear from you and yes a donation would be right.

Regards

Mr James Joseph

From: Bob Servant
To: James Joseph
Subject: Let's Do It!

James,
That's terrific. Right well let's plan for this Sunday then for the first meeting of the Church Of Broughty Ferry. I'd better start hunting for a suitable

40 See *Dundee Yellow Pages*, p.26, Bakeries, 'A Pie for A Pie', 176 Clepington Road (closed Sundays).

location. What does a church need please, James? I've seen them on Songs Of Praise but I know that's all CGI.[41] And how can I get people along on Sunday? Give me some bait for my Jesus hook.

Can I also please take this opportunity to say that I really appreciate you doing this for me. As it says in the bible, 'You will meet a tall, dark stranger'. Well I think I've met mine! Welcome aboard, James.

Bob Servant
Minister, Priest and Social Secretary
The Church Of Broughty Ferry

From: James Joseph
To: Bob Servant
Subject: My advice

Hello Bob,
I do not think it says this in the bible but do not worry on this. Yes this Sunday will be best Bob that is the day when God is most close. Bob, you can go and look for a building that has an open space that will contain at least 300 to 500 population. It must be near the commercial centre to attract the people. Bob I think people I in scottland will know God from you soon and this to to be success.

Mr. Bob for this donation I sugest that i am going to send you some of the living bible books to empower you so that you will know what to tell your congregations. I want this book to get to your door step at least by Sunday morning. This books will cost you $120 only, and you will get as many as 30 of this books to realy equip you in your ministry over there in your country for you to understand the bilble and how to apply the principle on it.

This the information to send the money.

NAME. REV. JAMES JOSEPH.
ADDRESS; LAGOS NIGERIA.
AMOUNT; $120 ONLY.
TEXT QUATIONS; BIBLE
TEXT ANSWER; CHURCH.

Rev. James Joseph.

N/B; jESUS IS LORD!

----

41 Some of the things that Bob has described to me as being 'all CGI': hovercrafts, the Grand National, the Eiffel Tower and the TV advertising campaigns of Domino's Pizza.

From: Bob Servant
To: James Joseph
Subject: Call off the search we have a church

Hi James,

The books sound like a good idea, put me down for 10 copies for now. OK, I have good news because I have found our church! I took your advice that it has to be near the commercial centre so had a wee walk down the High Street. The good news is that I found a building, the bad news is that it's the public toilet.

A couple of years ago Dundee City Council passed a law that everyone had to have a toilet in their house. Apart from a few conscientious objectors[42] most folk got on board so the public toilet doesn't really see much action these days. The only person that uses it is Slim Smith. I don't know if you know much about Slim Smith but he's the biggest guy in Broughty Ferry by quite some distance. I'm not entirely sure how much the guy weighs but I know that he's not measured in normal ways. What's a tonne, James? I think it might be a tonne. Or a fathom? I'm not sure. But the guy's the size of a two-berth caravan.

Anyway Slim is the only boy that uses the public toilet when he gets 'into trouble' as he puts it. I popped into Doc Ferry's bar earlier and Slim was in there with Chick Devine and Pop Wood. Slim promised me he's not going to be in town on Sunday so we're welcome to use the toilet for our church.

The toilet itself is quite small. There are three urinals, a couple of cubicles, some taps and so on. I was thinking that I'll put a plank over the sinks and stand up there, and the urinals could be a religious water feature. There's a nice high roof and with the tiling the hymns should sound wonderful.

I was also thinking, James, that a toilet is surely quite appropriate? The people in Dundee are full of the devil's poison and I have to get it out of their body in the same way you get things out of your body at the toilet. It is God that will push the poison out which I guess means Jesus is the toilet paper to clean up afterwards and I suppose I am the hand holding the toilet paper if you like. Do you follow, more or less, what I'm saying?

---

42 Bob learnt the phrase 'conscientious objectors' from a World War I documentary and uses it with great abandon, usually to 'conscientiously object' to something he has been asked to do. Off the top of my head, I have witnessed Bob 'conscientiously object' to: buying his round in Stewpot's Bar if he has not been the main contributor to the conversation, speaking to strangers at parties, giving up his seat on the bus to elderly women and paying the VAT applied to the cover price of a pornographic magazine.

Maybe I'm not making myself clear James and I apologise if that's the case. As it says in the bible 'You don't have to be mad to work here, but it helps!!!!'

Photo of the Church attached, it needs a wee tidy but as I said it ticks all the boxes

Bob Servant
Head Honcho
The Church of Broughty Ferry

From: James Joseph
To: Bob Servant
Subject: You must buy bibles

Bob
Yes like yo say you must tidy up this room properly for use Sunday. This is good that there is to be a church but be careful about the toilet because God name must always be used in place with respect. There is no mention of this being mad situation in bible Bob you are saying it wrong again. you might have different bible to me. that is why you buy must books from me to make sure you are equip with right bible for the scottland people.

remember about the books. If i can have the money today i believe you can get the parcel at your doorstep first thing monday morning through Express courier services DHL. You have all payment detail.

Rev. James Joseph

From: Bob Servant
To: James Joseph
Subject: Up to four!

Hi James,
Thanks for giving the toilet the nod and don't worry I'll give it a wee tidy later. Right, things are heating up here ahead of tomorrow's first congregation of the Church of Broughty Ferry. I'm very pleased to say I have three confirmed guests. They are:

My neighbour and best pal Frank. Frank used to work for me on the windowcleaning and the burger vans so I suppose you can say he's been a disciple for a few years. He's Judassed me on a few occasions, I'm not going to deny it, but he's also been my Moses when I've needed him. I think we can trust him, James, and I'm giving him the vice-captain position.

Tommy Peanuts. Tommy's an old pal of mine and he's struggling to come to terms with his divorce from his wife. Believe it or not she left him in 1987 for a guy with a Fiat Corsa and a nice line in sarcasm but things are as bad as ever so I thought he should come along and hear what God has to say about things.

Mrs Henderson. She's a game old bird who I met at Safeways tonight. She's quite blind but but we had a good chat and she clearly still knows what side the bread's buttered on so I invited her along. It'll be good to have some skirt there anyway.

I know it's not the best turnout in the world James but, as it says in the bible, 'three's a crowd'.

Right I need to get this sermon written for tomorrow, better go.

Bob

From: James Joseph
To: Bob Servant
Subject: Bibles

Bob

You did not even mention bibles i have them heer for you all agreed? Wheers is the money for these book bob you promised are you not religous man like you said? you show again that you are using the wrong bible with these words

Yes three people is ok for now – out of seeds grow bigger plants bob this is what to remember. A sermon is always needed of course best to speak to people hearts bob and have them find connection of their own with God.

Send money for bibles and i can have them rush job to you DHL

James

From: Bob Servant
To: James Joseph
Subject: The Sermon

Hi James,
OK I've had a shot at the sermon and I am very proud to send you the attached. I hope you like it because I think it presses all the right buttons. As Jesus says in the bible 'I'm happy as Larry'.

That's me off to bed ahead of the big day tomorrow. I will dream of Jesus (not in a saucy way). I hope you have a good night. May God be with you (not in a saucy way).

Bob

THE CHURCH OF BROUGHTY FERRY

OPENING SERMON BY PASTOR BOB SERVANT,
'THE PEOPLE'S PASTOR'

Ladies and Gentlemen, thank you for coming to
the debut congregation of the 'all new' Church
of Broughty Ferry. You know, a lot of people
ask me about God. They ask about who he is and
what he wants. Well, let me tell you this. God
is a man who has seen it all. He has heard
every joke, told every story and spent time
with some of the most interesting people in
the world. To keep it simple, God is like
Nelson Mandela or the former Grandstand
presenter Bob Wilson.

Bob Wilson, ladies and gentlemen, wasn't a
trained television presenter and a lot of
people forget that. He was a goalie and a
pretty decent one as well. He played for
Scotland but I think he only got one cap, I
can't remember. But when he hung up the gloves
Bob Wilson didn't spend his time swaggering
round the golf club or acting the big shot at
the swimming baths. No, Bob Wilson got the bus
to the BBC, picked up a microphone and said
'Can I have a wee shot at this lads?' And the
rest is history.

Like Bob Wilson, God is a man of many jobs. He
helps people with problems, he stops wars and
he makes sure that everyone in the world gets
their dinner. And just when you thought he
couldn't do any more, God had sex with Mary and
produced the twins — Joseph and Jesus. Those
twins were not just two adorable wee lads,
which they were, they also went about the
business of telling people about God and not
in a 'Oh you should see my Dad he's a cowboy
during the week and an astronaut at the
weekend' sort of way. But in a 'My Dad's God,
beat that' sort of way which was fair enough
and not as arrogant as it might sound. When

Joseph retired and Jesus was murdered by the Nazis, God had a wee cry, shook himself down and kept going and he's still going strong today.

A lot of people ask me how old God is. I tell them to think of the biggest number they know then double it and add 32 and that's not how old God is, that's how old his NEWEST pair of trainers are. God is the oldest man in the world and, as long as he stays alive, it's going to very hard for anyone to nick that title off him. And here's the twist, if someone did become older than him, then God would be the first boy at their door with a chocolate orange and a birthday card because that's the kind of boy he is. He's a nice guy, that's what I'm saying, ladies and gentleman, more than anything. God is a nice guy. Nicer than anyone you know. He's nicer than Gloria Hunniford and, yes, he's nicer than the Pope who, let's not forget, works for God. If God is a newsagent, and a lot of people say he is, then the Pope is God's paperboy.

Ladies and Gentlemen, thank you for listening and let me leave you with this. Who made those clothes you are wearing? The cardigans, the duffel coats and the underpants? Don't read the label. Read your hearts. Because your clothes, ladies and gentlemen, were made by God and he didn't even tell you. That is the kind of guy he is. Good morning, ladies and gentleman. Follow God's path and watch the step on the way out because Frank tripped on it the other day and went down like the Belgrano.

Good afternoon ladies and gentlemen. Hallejulah! See you in heaven. I love you. Come back next week, there will be a collection for those who can afford it, good night and Amen.

(APPLAUSE)

Page 2

From: James Joseph
To: Bob Servant
Subject: Sermon OK

Bob this is all fine you talk well off god tho maybe it is little confusing
with the other people but god is there and this is fine and yes it is right for
hallejulahg and to end everything with the AMEN.

It is Sunday now bob and you have not bought the bibles so this is very
rong and you musst know this too bob. ok well let us say the bibbles will
be with you next week and then you will be ready to go through with the
second meeting of your new CHURCH.

Good luck today bob let me kno if the great sucess i know it will be
and then you can send the money for the bibles OK Bob.

GOOD LUCK

Rev. James Joseph

From: Bob Servant
To: James Joseph
Subject: I'm Having Doubts

James,

Well, where to begin? It's fair to say that the Church of Broughty Ferry
didn't go exactly as you and I had hoped. It started not too bad. Tommy,
Frank and Mrs Henderson all showed up and I stood outside the toilet and
welcomed them with a bit of a pat on the back and some of the 'God Be
With You' stuff. I made a wee joke about the steps up to the toilet being
our 'Stairway to Heaven' and the atmosphere was pretty decent when I
climbed up onto the taps for the sermon.

Unfortunately I had just started my speech when Slim Smith came
into the toilet. He didn't say anything and none of the others saw him. He
just shook his head and went straight into a cubicle. I was knocked off my
stride but for a moment it seemed like we'd get away it.

Then he started. James, the noises that Slim made were simply
inhumane. What came out of that cubicle sounded like a drunken brass
band. Unfortunately at the first blast from the cubicle Mrs Henderson
thought it was the opening note of Onward Christian Soldiers and started
singing away, which got Frank started. They barely knew the words so
trying to match their singing up to Slim's 'tune' was a tough job for them.
Then Tommy Peanuts started crying which I thought was because of his
divorce but was actually because he was standing nearest the cubicle.

In the end I had to climb down from the sinks and lead the congregation
outside. Mrs Henderson said I should sack my organist and stormed
off, Tommy went away to drown his sorrows and me and Frank waited

for Slim. He finally came out looking very sorry for himself and said he'd had an entire pork belly for breakfast. Frank tried to lighten the mood by saying that at least Slim had 'made a donation' but I told Frank it was not a laughing matter and walked away with my head held high but my heart feeling like a lava lamp.

That's me back at the house now, James, and I just don't know what to say. What kind of God would allow this to happen? What kind of God would convince Slim Smith to eat an entire pork belly for breakfast? I just don't know any more, James. I'm wondering that maybe there is no God after all and we've both been duped?

Yours In Doubt,

Bob

**From: James Joseph
To: Bob Servant
Subject: RE: I'm Having Doubts**

Bob I start to think you are for joking because this is just too extreme now. a man went to the toilet in the church and this made a man cry and everything go bust? Come on bob this is not right it cannot be for true.

If you are real and this is what you are really doing in scottland then show me by sending the money today for your books and do not let me down bob because i already have the books from the printers and they are packed and all ready nice for you

James

**From: Bob Servant
To: James Joseph
Subject: Hold Tight!**

James,
I have had a message from God and Jesus! I was sitting down for breakfast having a wee think about how maybe all the God stuff is bollocks when I picked up my banana and, well, you just wouldn't believe it James. My eyes aren't as good as they used to be but if you hold the banana in a certain light and kind of screw your eyes up it looks a little bit like Jesus. Maybe I'm wrong, but I nearly choked to death on my Shreddies. Can you see anything?

Yours in Hope,

Bob

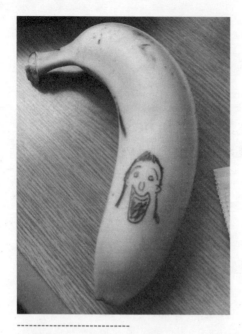

NO REPLY

14

The Skirt Hunt and the Dunblane Hydro

From: Elena Denisov
To: Bob Servant
Subject: To me you are love

To my dear,
Do not be surprised to hear from me. I look for love from men in your country and you were advised for me to contact as man of great honour. I want to tell to you it is a little about itself. I live in city Obst and I have very good family. Because of my work I take off a small apartment and I live in it separately from my family. But I very much frequently reach to them and I spend with them weekend. now I work as the senior seller in shop store, which sells female footwear.

My work brings to me not so many money, but it is pleasant to me. I very much like to laugh and I respect the people with good humour. I like to travel. I yet was not far from mine At home, but I dream in the future to visit in different places. I 2-3 times in Week go to be engaged in sports hall, to hold my body in The order. And you. It will be very interesting to me to learn about it. I wait for your letters.

Sincerely yours,

Elena

From: Bob Servant
To: Elena Denisov
Subject: Cupid Must Be Wondering Where His Arrow Is Because It's Sticking Out My Fucking Head

Elena,

Thanks very much for getting in touch and I'm very glad that you did. Looking at your photo made my eyes feel like they were on all expenses paid holiday to the Costa Del Skirt. I should tell you right off the bat that I am 64 years old. That doesn't mean that I'm not active on the skirt front but I know that for some skirt I might have too many miles on the clock. That's frankly ridiculous because you can't put a price on experience, just look at Bryan Ferry or that bird from Murder She Wrote.

If I was to start telling you, Elena, about all the adventures I've had with skirt then we'd be here all night so let me just say that if someone wrote a book about skirt then under every category there would be a wee number to go to the index and then the entire index would just say 'Ask Bob Servant'. They reckon when you die that your whole life flashes before your eyes. Well I'll just see one long piece of skirt with Frank's voice over the top asking for money. That's not much of a way to die is it? It's not exactly Butch Cassidy going 'all in' with the Mexicans.

So maybe you're the answer Elena. What a pair we could be. Like Torvill and Dean with extra sauce, or Cannon and Ball with less. Sorry, I mean more. Although the thought of a sauce-heavy Cannon and Ball is the stuff of nightmares, as I'm sure you'd agree?

I live in Scotland but you should know that I'm not one of those boys who abuses women by giving them cruel nicknames or making fun of their walks. For a start I'd have the local branch of the Skirt Protection League on my back but that's not what would stop me. I'm a romantic, Elena, it's as simple as that.

I attach a photo of my house for your records,

Your Servant,

Bob Servant

43

From: Elena Denisov
To: Bob Servant
Subject: This age is fine

Dear bob

Have good day? I waited your letter and was very much Is pleased, when you have written to me. I am waiting for your letters every day! we begin to learn each other more well and to develop Our acquaintance. I think, that it is an interesting thing, to learn someone far through the Internet. It is unusual to me, because I a little is familiar with the Internet.

Your age is not mean anything to me at bob so just forget this. At 64 this is till young with the medicines availables today and this is OK for me

---

43 This isn't Bob's house. In fact, it's the oriental-inspired home of Coldplay bass guitar player Guy 'Fife' Berryman which fairly dominates central Kirkcaldy. *This photo copyright © Scottish Celebrity Homes Magazine ltd.*

if you have known many women because I excpect this from a man of 64 and this is just experience like you say. your house so beautiful and way you respect and not abuse women is only joy to me bob.

My heart sing that you reply. I am so happy to hear from you back. Bob i understand that you are looking for wife if you sure if what you are saying i will agree to come your country or can you come down to my country because you know i have nobody to take care of me here.

Ok bob i must go now to work in the shoe store. with all my love

Elena

From: Bob Servant
To: Elena Denisov
Subject: The Hydro

Hi Elena,

Sorry for the delay in getting back to you. It's just that Wimbledon has kicked off and as always I am throwing in my lot with Andy Murray. I call him 'The Dunblane Hydro'[44] which always gets a good reception in the boozers round here.

I'm a big tennis fan, Elena, it's ideally suited to my mentality because it's a battle of wits and I've got more wits than all the other boys round here put together. Before you ask, yes I have 'swung the strings' in my time. My God, Elena, you should have seen me out on the court when I was younger. I had a serve that could cause blindness, a second serve I called 'Old Faithful' and a backhand slice that started whispers as far north as Arbroath.

These days the knees won't join in like they used to so I just stick on my white shorts and my headband then sit down, pour myself a well deserved OVD and watch the Dunblane Hydro.

And why not?

Yours in sport,

Bob

---

44 This is the name of a well-known hotel in Andy Murray's hometown of Dunblane. I vividly remember the day that Bob came up with this nickname for Murray, due to the seven text messages he sent me. The first message contained the nickname, the second to fifth messages read 'What do you think?' and were sent at roughly one-minute intervals, the sixth message read 'It's a hotel in Dunblane where he's from', and the seventh message read 'Only use it if you say it's mine'. I received all seven messages together when I emerged from a torturous journey on the London Underground and was very tempted to go straight back down the steps.

PS I attach a photo of the Hydro. Look at those eyes, Elena. It's like Boris Becker has taken them out of their sockets, polished them up and put them back in.

From: Elena Denisov
To: Bob Servant
Subject: Tennis player

hello.

ok bob this andy murray is a professional tennis player and the current British numbers one. This is ok for you to have a hobby and sport that you like and watch because i want you to have many intrests and stay active and this will make your life much longer than the 64.

bob i am wondering what the plan would be for us. my problem is to have somebody in my life and you are promising that you are need of a wife and am here to be your fucture patner. please are you realy need a wife if that get back to me with your mind and let's move forward in this our relationship waiting to here from you again.

You tell me how you are with women bob so i should know bob how I am with men. I respect them always and i can't find something that will makes me embarass a man infront of his friends. i can also cook what ever you will like me to cook for you.

Bob i am a little worried about my job. it is not customers at the shoe store and sometimes i wonder if all will be ok. I send another photo to you Bob.

Elena

From: Bob Servant
To: Elena Denisov
Subject: Gone Fishin'

Elena,

Looking at these photos of you makes me feel like I am on a timeshare in a log cabin next to a lake full of love fish. I want to walk out of the cabin, throw my hook of truth in the water, reel you in, gut you, lightly smoke you over a fire made out of lust, cover you in a sauce of desire and then absolutely devour you.

It's also great to hear that you won't embarrass me in front of my pals, particularly because that is actually a crime here in Scotland.[45] I'm sorry to hear business is a bit slow at the shoe store but I'm sure it will pick up. At the end of the day, Elena, people still have feet. I'd like to see the

---

45 See *Female Conduct in Public Spaces (Scotland) Act 2010, Section 1, Part IX*: 'Females will not deliberately embarrass their partners in any public area where their partner is within ten metres of a known associate.' Also see *The Scotsman*, 16 April 2010: *'Scottish Parliament Defends "Skirt Laws"'*. ('"American TV shows and the Internet have caused confusion amongst the nation's skirt," said a Parliament spokesman. "These should be seen as gentle reminders from an old friend."')

Government try and make cutbacks in the number of feet we're allowed. There would be a riot and they'd only have themselves to blame. Maybe suggest to your boss that you do a bit of team-building but be careful. I remember when I tried to get the atmosphere going on the cheeseburger vans with a 'Bring a Kid to Work Day' but that backfired when Frank got done on kidnapping charges.

I'm glad you're on the ball with the Dunblane Hydro. You'll have seen that he's now swept a couple of numpties aside. I reckon that German boy was there to cut the grass and just picked up a racquet for a laugh. I do worry a wee bit about the heat though. The Hydro's from Dunblane and they're asking him to play in a hundred bloody degrees. You should have seen him after the game, Elena, he looked like he'd been for a pint on the surface of the sun.

Yours,

Bob

From: Elena Denisov
To: Bob Servant
Subject: This age is fine

Hi bob

I admire your story from the lake. yes i feel all this too bob. desire and lust and even it is right to talk about love because i think this is love we are entering also. We talk so freely like this is something that we have done since time begins. Bob do you experience also this feelings? I think about you all time bob, when i eat and dress and work at the shoe store and from my way between. Every hour you arrive into my head and i am pleased to have you do this! Please tell me this is not me alone in this thought bob.

I am glad about your Murray hydro win. You must be the best fan bob to make him win like this! If he wins the competition then he should know it is because of fans like you bob.

So bob we should work out master plans to bring us together. Two options are clear bob that you come here or me to you. i will speak to the government department for me to come to your home i might have to buy small visa bob will let you know this.

Bob you must be senting me your photo soon i only know you through words,

Elena

From: Bob Servant
To: Elena Denisov
Subject: Frank's on the case

Elena,

Another good win for the Hydro today eh? The kid's got it, there's no doubt about that.

Anyway, you're right we need to see each other. I was down at the Cuckoo's Nest bar earlier chatting to Terry Darcus and Big Sandy about this and then my neighbour Frank (who wasn't strictly involved in the conversation) chipped in with an idea that made me stand up like a totem pole. What he says he's going to do, Elena, is build a telescope in his garden that will let me see you.

I asked if he was sure I'd be able to see Russia from Broughty Ferry and he said we should be fine as long as it's not too windy. I'm very excited about this, Elena, and also very proud of Frank. He used to work for me selling cheeseburgers on my vans but if he pulls this off then he could be one of the great Scottish inventors like Alexander Graham Bell.[46]

I don't know if you know much about Alexander Graham Bell but he was the Scottish scientist big gun who invented the telephone. It was back when most of the other scientist big guns were experimenting with trannies.[47] Bell experimented with trannies a little bit (mostly in his shed when his wife was out at work) but after a wee while of messing about with trannies[48] and trying on their lipstick, Bell had enough of them and decided to invent the telephone.

So as soon as Frank's finished building his telescope we should be able to see each other fine. I can't wait. I'm going to give a big 'Dundee hello' to you and then my old pal Baz who lives in France, before Tommy Peanuts wants to borrow the telescope to check on his ex wife, then Nipper Kolacz wants to borrow it for God knows what.

I've attached a photo of myself as requested. I'm a little shy as you can see, but I hope you think I look handsome?

Bob

---

46 Bell, Alexander Graham (1847–1922). Edinburgh-born inventor of the telephone. See *The Dundee Courier*, 4 August 1876: *'Edinburgh Man Builds Snooping Machine'*.
47 Scottish slang for radios.
48 Again, Scottish slang for radios.

From: Elena Denisov
To: Bob Servant
Subject: This will not work

Bob

But this is not the plan bob how can you think it is. Your friend will not have the qualities to build a telescope for you to see from Scotland to Russia bob it is far too far. In fact i do not think this is something that could be built by scientists and men of study so if your friend works sales cheeseburgers then how could he do this. Come on bob stay real and think again of how we can see.

Well i have some news of this. I have been to the correct government department and i can purchase a visa to visit you for $1400. I went straight to the travel company and there can be a flight from here to you in Scotland Bob for just $1600 so this is $3000. I have some terrible news today bob that the shoe store is closing down because of no business. I am a women of belief that i am equal to man so wish I could buy this package bob but right now I am stuck and can not because the shoe store close down.

Can you send this money today bob? Bob you should not be so shy! Send a proper photo and yes i am ever glad about your Hydro Murray bob. you show a lot of support for this man and this is one reason why there is love from me for your loyalty bob.

Your love

Elena

From: Bob Servant
To: Elena Denisov
Subject: Forget the Telescope

Good Evening Elena,
You're probably right, the telescope was a bit pie in the sky (no pun intended). I went and spoke to Frank earlier and said that you're going to fly over to Scotland instead. He said he would build an airport in his garden for you to land in but I said that wasn't necessary.

OK let me have a think about you coming to Scotland. The only slight problem is the Hydro. I am finding myself thinking about him all the time and I just don't know if I could give you the attention that you deserve.

That's the Hydro through to the semi finals to play the Spanish boy and I've spent all morning planning a party. Me and the boys are putting together one of the biggest buffets that Broughty Ferry's ever seen. I'm cooking up Meat Attack Cheeseburgers, Frank's bringing a wheelbarrow full of chips, Chappy Williams and Tommy Peanuts are bringing a briefcase full of chicken wings and Slim Smith is bringing a bib.

We've made a few banners:

'Welcome to the Dunblane Hydro, Your Checkout Time is RIGHT NOW'.

'The Pain in Spain Falls Mainly on Nadal's Brain'.

'Welcome to Andy Murray's Spanish Restaurant. Dishes are "Served" Hot'!

This is the big one, Elena. I attach a photo of a Meat Attack for your records.

Yours,

Bob

From: Elena Denisov
To: Bob Servant
Subject: Who is it you love bob me or hydro?

Bob I wonder if you can give me more attention than your favourite Murray or Hydro because it seems this is all you talk about? Now you say you think about him more than you think of me what is wrong with you Bob this is not the way?

From: Bob Servant
To: Elena Denisov
Subject: My Darkest Hour

Elena,
The Hydro got beat. I can hardly lift my fingers to the keyboard, Elena. When I see my hands I just think, 'the Hydro has hands too' and then I start crying like Harry Secombe has sat on my cat.

Yours in utter devastation,

Bob

From: Elena Denisov
To: Bob Servant
Subject: Be a proper man

Bob this is too much what is wrong with you you are 64 man and you are this sad because of a tennis? bob there is other tennis chances for the Hydro Murray and you will be alive to watch them. But this is just the chance you have with me bob, only one. And now you are danger because the chance could be gone just because of your feelings for the hydro murray player do you see bob? this is not right and you must see the sense very quick now bob before it is all too late.

From: Bob Servant
To: Elena Denisov
Subject: My Decision

Elena,
This is the hardest email I've written since I switched from Scottish Gas to British Gas which, considering their advertising campaign, took a lot of soul searching.[49] First I would like to thank you for the opportunity you have given me to make the choice between you and the Dunblane Hydro.

I have now given it some serious thought. On the one side there is some wonderful hair, come to bed eyes and legs to die for. On the other side is you. On the one hand there are strong forearms, great movement and an amazing collection of headbands. On the other is the Dunblane Hydro.

It was a tough choice Elena, a hell of a choice, but I have made it. I'm sorry Elena but I choose the Hydro. There's something about the kid. I choose the Hydro.

My God, Elena, I'm crying as if my granny has just announced that she's going out with Mathew Kelly.

I choose the Hydro, Elena. In the name of love I choose the Hydro.

Your Servant,

Bob Servant

----

49 See *The Scotsman*, 27 March 2011: '*Scottish Gas Reprimanded for Anti-English Campaign*' ('Scottish Gas was fined today for an advertising campaign which suggested that British Gas generated their gas "from the tears of Scottish orphans"').

From: Elena Denisov
To: Bob Servant
Subject: RE My Decision

Bob you cannot be making this choice what is wrong with you. Think again bob and be quick.

15
The Vanishing Beard

From: Alistair Ross
To: Bob Servant
Subject: Do Not Ignore This

Dear Respected Sir,

I got your contact email address through internet research as i was conducting researches to link-up a reliable foreign partner to help me carry out this transaction. On coming accross your contact, i was touched spiritually and physically to connect you, with great feelings that you might be of great help to me.

I live here in Australia and work for the Australia Investments Corp. To be very honest with you, this business i have introduced to you is very genuine and highly benefitial. i have the absolute convinction that you will neither betray nor disappoint me in this transaction. I have access to a fund which if is not claimed after eight years it will enter into the bank's treasury and becomes the inherittance of the Australian government but instead I could transfer to you.

If this sounds like what you want and need then contacts me right away. Please trust in me just as i have trusted you before opening the secret of this business to you because about 99.9% of all genuine transactions all over the world is based on mutual trust and understanding. You will see the form to fill in here.

Thanks and best regards

Alistair Ross
Australia Investments Corp

From: Bob Servant
To: Alistair Ross
Subject: Quick snap?

Hi Alistair,

Sounds great, can you please send a photo of yourself for my records?

Your Servant,

Bob Servant

From: Alistair Ross
To: Bob Servant
Subject: This is no problem

Hello bob yes this is no problem for photo here is me in my private office. Ok well now we can procede?

From: Bob Servant
To: Alistair Ross
Subject: Let's lose the beard

Morning champ,
OK here's my position. I don't like beards, Alistair, I don't like them at all. About forty years ago I saw a documentary about a guy with a beard who led a gang of young pickpockets in London and then one of the kids started singing as if someone had his little balls in a vice and, oh dear, the whole thing was awful.[50]

---

50 I think Bob is referring to the 1968 film adaptation of *Oliver Twist* and specifically to the part of Fagin and the singing of the 9-year-old lead actor, Mark Lester. My take on Lester's voice would be far more charitable. I think that Lester, who in later life would become godfather to Michael Jackson's children (this is true), sang like an angel.

So Alistair, it's very simple. Simply shave off your beard and sit back in that same chair in that same office and send me a new photo. I will then send you every single penny I have as well as my neighbour Frank's pension book and 'flat screen' TV.

Because, don't get me wrong, Alistair, I can see your potential. You, Alistair, are wearing a sandwich board saying 'Opportunity', a top hat saying 'Trust Me' and, if I may, a pair of pants embroidered with the phrase 'Work Hard' at the front and, if I may, 'Play Hard', at the back.

That last bit was all metaphors.

Look forward to seeing the new photo,

Bob

From: Alistair Ross
To: Bob Servant
Subject: I cannot do this

Bob,
I cannot do this because my wife likes my beard and in fact it was her idea. If you're married man then this will work for you. Just fill in the form or if you want to send your whole money for investment purposes this is fine too. I do not need your friend TV I have one that is doing OK. Thank you for the metaphor i get message and you right this is 'OPPORTUNITY' and i will so hard for you you will be amazed.

Alistair

From: Bob Servant
To: Alistair Ross
Subject: Stand up to her

Alistair,
Don't let your wife be your boss. You'll end up like the Duke of Edinburgh who has to ask the Queen before he goes to the toilet.[51] So I apologise to you and your dragon of a wife, Alistair, but if you want to do business then the beard has to go.

Bob

---

51 I can't imagine that the 90-year-old Duke of Edinburgh asks permission from the Queen to visit the bathroom. However, if her Majesty does enforce such a rule then, as always, she will have done so for the nation's wellbeing and in the spirit of the Blitz.

From: Alistair Ross
To: Bob Servant
Subject: Not important

Bob,
The beard does not matter in business bob you must know this. Send your information anyway.

Alistair

From: Bob Servant
To: Alistair Ross
Subject: Goodbye

Alistair,
I have made my position clear. Until I see the photo as requested I will be playing deaf to your emails.

Goodbye,

Bob

From: Alistair Ross
To: Bob Servant
Subject: Trust me

Bob
Come on this is not important and why does photo have to be the same. You don't trust me! bob why not? Send the information.

Alistair

From: Alistair Ross
To: Bob Servant
Subject: Answer me

Bob? not heard from you, send something today.

From: Alistair Ross
To: Bob Servant
Subject: OK here it is

OK Bob here is photo like you ask, I have removed my beard even if it causes problem with my wife. Now send your data now or if you want whole money invested I have many opportunities that you will like.

From: Bob Servant
To: Alistair Ross
Subject: RE: OK here it is

Please tell me that you're joking.

From: Alistair Ross
To: Bob Servant
Subject: Of course not a joke

Bob this is business not joking what is problem?

From: Bob Servant
To: Alistair Ross
Subject: Have a guess

What do you think the problem might be?

From: Alistair Ross
To: Bob Servant
Subject: RE: Have a guess

i really do not know bob can you send me your details to arrange
investment?

From: Bob Servant
To: Alistair Ross
Subject: Come on Alistair

Alistair,
If you said you were joking, I would have all the respect in the world for you.

Bob

From: Alistair Ross
To: Bob Servant
Subject: OK

ok i am joking does that help?

From: Bob Servant
To: Alistair Ross
Subject: Love

Alistair,
I may, I repeat may, have fallen in love with you,

Bob

NO REPLY

16

Deadeye the Fleet-footed Wonderboy

From: Chris Adams
To: Bob Servant
Subject: Can you help?

Dear Sir / Madam Please read.

It is my sincere pleasure at this moment to exhibit my total trust bestowed on you in accordance to my Proposed partnership relationship with you of which I am fully convinced that you will really welcome my partner. It is my Godly nursed intention to prove myself to you that I am very much different from others which you must have come across on the Internet.

The truth is that I am a dying man looking to invest funds abroad for the sake of my children and grandchildren. You are a business or invididual that i have picked as a possible receiver of this investment. Simply return how much you would require and why i will consider how we can proceed. The money would come by banking transfer so let us save time by you providing full banking dretails on the form below.

1) Your Full Name........................... ...
2) Your Age........................... ....
3) Your Mobile and Home Phone Number..............
4) Your Fax Number....................…....
5) Your Country of Nationality..................…............. .
6) Your Occupation................... ....
7) Sex........................... ....
8) Alternative E-mail Address/ ....

I look forward for your immediate Positive response.
My regards to you and the family,

Mr Chris Adams

From: Bob Servant
To: Chris Adams
Subject: Too Busy

Hello Chris,

Thanks for getting in touch and I'm sorry to hear that you're having a tough time. I'm afraid I can't help you right now as I am extremely busy. I feel like Santa on Christmas Eve or Dundee A&E on Christmas Day.[52]

I am Head Scout with a Scottish football team called Dundee United and I'm busy trying to find a star signing for the new season. We've lost a few players and the natives are restless. I need to pull something big out of my cat[53] here, Chris, a real Bobby Dazzler who can show the opposition a clean pair of heels and have the punters up on their tiptoes waving their rattles and with smiles as wide as the Clyde. I've got a bit of money to spend on the right player and, by God, I intend to get him.

Sorry Chris, I don't know why I'm telling you all this. You're busy with your health problems.

Best of luck for the future,

Your Servant,

Bob Servant

From: Chris Adams
To: Bob Servant
Subject: I know a star player

Bob,

In fact bob you are in most luck right now because I know a football soccer player like you will not believe. I am weak but I can work on you with this if i was to introduce. Then of course you pay a fee. say $5000 as lump sum to be paid now?

This player is one of the best that you will have seen. He has multiple experience and like you say will cause joy to the people. I myself have seen him play many times and in fact has been great comfort to me during illness to watch him play that is how much beautiful it is.

Chris

---

52 See *The Dundee Courier*, 26 December 2010: *'Christmas Calamities'* (' "All I'd ask him is 'Was it really worth it?' " said one middle-aged woman whose right foot had been crudely superglued to a turkey').
53 Hat, presumably.

From: Bob Servant
To: Chris Adams
Subject: We don't pay agents

Chris,

That's a stroke of luck. Sorry we are not paying agents just now because of the cutbacks but I'm sure you'll want your friend to have his shot at glory and I'd imagine he'll chuck a few quid your way. Put it this way, he'll be getting a package like you wouldn't believe. We pay wages, expenses and a £50 a month boot polish allowance so I'm sure he'll bung you a fiver or two.

Yours,

Bob

From: Chris Adams
To: Bob Servant
Subject: I will pass this on

OK Bob I will pass you on and you can pay him money. Yes I will arrange with him. His name is Don Woodward and he will be in touch soon. I believe that he is even at training right now so this is a good sign for you Bob.

From: Don Woodward
To: Bob Servant
Subject: I am a striker with excellent experience

Dear Mr. Bob Servant The Chief player Scout
Good day Sir. I am pleased to write to inform you of my intention to ask that you give me an offer and a place in your Scottish football team of DUNDEE UNITED. I was given your details by one of my fans CHRIS ADAMS.

well what to say. I will keep short for now. I am a striker with excellent experience, young, strong & have good pace, very skillful and intelligent on the ball. It would be quite right for me to have a place at your football club. I have played for a number of top professional club here in Africa including leage champions and cup winner.

I am happy to come and play for your team overe in Scotland and this is fine. I wil have to arrange release here and then there are all the costs to come to you and this will be quite high.

So let us arrange a deal and soon i will be there playing for you with all my heart Bob

thank you and pleased to meet you bob

DON WOODWARD
Football Player. Position: Forward

From: Bob Servant
To: Don Woodward
Subject: You're ticking my boxes

Don,

Thanks for getting in touch. You sound like a strong possibility. One slight hitch is that I've just had a wee look online for your name and could not find it anywhere. Considering the fact that you've played for league champions, that made my eyebrows take off like helicopters.

I presume you can clear this up easily enough? I certainly hope so. The fans want a star signing and there's a really terrible atmosphere around the place. I've not seen Dundee like this since the Timex strike which was a bad time for the city. Well, to be fair, it was a pretty good time for me.[54]

Your Servant,

Bob Servant
Chief Scout

From: Don Woodward
To: Bob Servant
Subject: Not Important

Dear Mr. Bob Chief Scout
Do not worry bob not all teams and leagues here bother to post their news on internet why would they? Most fans know of the teams and players

---

54 The Timex Strike of 1993 thrust Dundee into the national consciousness. When the Timex company brought in 'scab' labour to break the strike there was the worst picket-line violence seen in Britain since the 1984 miners' strike. As Bob said, however, not everyone in the city suffered during the strike. See *The Dundee Courier*, 10 January 1993: *'Dundee Cheese Burger Van Mogul Defends Timex Relocation'* ('"I greatly admire the strikers and I am here to help," said Servant (46) who has been selling large quantities of fast food to the crowd outside the factory gates. Servant pointed out that he has incurred significant costs "rebranding" his van. He now offers the "Scargill Sandwich" (a cheeseburger), the "Bolshevik Burger" (a cheeseburger) and "Stalin's Surprise" (also a cheeseburger). Servant went on to defend his offer of high-interest credit to the strikers which he is marketing under the banner "Bash the Scabs, Start a Tab!" ').

through word of mouth and this is how you have come to hear of me so you are in fact the evidence against yourself.

If you need more information then you should just come and ask me bob instead of wasting your time on the computer. You should know that I am 18 years old and am well built, very strong in air and very good on fifty fifty balls. I have speed and can beat defenders very easily and score with the help of my inborn speed. Also i am very skillful and intelligent on the ball.

My position is forward, in my previous club i play as the top striker and due get result for my team. I am 6 foot 3 tall.

Regards

Don Woodward
Football Player. Position: Forward

From: Bob Servant
To: Don Woodward
Subject: Your New Name

Don,

Wasting time on the computer is one thing that I hope no one can ever accuse me of. Right, my friend, things are looking good. The first thing I need to do, of course, is give you a new name. It is absolutely vital over here that any star player we have is given a name that will have the fans giving it laldy on their way to the ground and then waving their scarves like lunatics when you take to the grass. Some of our old heroes here at United had great names. I'm thinking, as you'll know, of boys like Slippers Malpas, Angel Toes Bannon and old 'Magic Socks' himself – Trickshot Narey The Man Who Made Physics Cry.

Anyway, I've had a think and this is what I want to call you:

Deadeye the Fleet-footed Wonderboy

OK with you? Thanks for all the information. Can I just check on things like diet and personality? Tell me a little about the real Deadeye.

I attach a photo of old Trickshot Narey. My God what a player he was,

Bob

From: Don Woodward
To: Bob Servant
Subject: Name OK

Dear Mr. Bob Servant

Thanks once again for you communication. OK i understand this with
the name and this is fine to call me. It is also correct as i am fleet foot for
sure. Bob i run like you will not believe. I like your picture and i hope i
can play as well as these famous names.

Regarding my character, i am humble and only concentrate on my
football carrier. I like listening to soft music and most of the American
gospels Music. Gospel songs is my daily bread that give me lots of
inspiration in my career. For diet I take lite food in the morning after
training and rice for my evening meals.

So it is good we are nearly in agreement. can we start to arrange our
deal now bob? i do not like to talk of these things i rather talk only of
football but the business must be done so let us carry on.

From Don, or for you it is DEADEYE!

From: Bob Servant
To: Don Woodward
Subject: Some action shots?

Deadeye,

I'm delighted to hear about the Gospel music and the rice, which is the
kind of combination I was hoping you'd come up with. Right well I think it's

time that I saw Deadeye in action. Can you send some photos from your latest training session please?

By God, Deadeye, I can't wait to see you with the ball at your feet, skipping past the opposition as if they were lampposts and then firing one into the old onion bag. You're my kind of player, Deadeye, and, more importantly, you're my kind of man. A man's man, if you like. You, Deadeye, are the kind of man that I could spend all day drinking with in a graveyard and then go home to the wife and she'd wipe the custard off her apron and say 'what did you do today then?' and I'd say 'today I met a man. That's all, I met a man'.

I literally cannot talk any higher of you than that. I'm so glad I met you Deadeye. You've really come up with the goods for me, like Nick Owen did when Sir Trevor McDonald poisoned that bus driver.[55]

Bob
Chief Scout

From: Don Woodward
To: Bob Servant
Subject: photos from training time

Bob

Thank you Bob I will never let you down when I play for you and i will never forget that you talk of me like this. I see this as respect between men and I will repay you for sure when I am on the pitch. Your wife is surely a best woman as well and i look forward to seeing her with you there in Scotland when i play my first game in fact i dedicate my first game to you and your family because of all you have done for me.

You want photos so i have sent some now from my training and they show well my capabties for you. You should know my TRAINING SCHEDULE:-

I do Gim on Saturdays evening but i train twice everyday from Monday–Friday. I like Physical training on Monday morning and lite ball

---

55 The former television newsreader Sir Trevor McDonald has never poisoned a bus driver. He did, however, beat a homeless man to death in Birmingham in 1991. See *Your Headlines Tonight: The Trevor McDonald Story* p.201 ('"Any change, Sir Trevor?" he asked. I looked around me. We were alone. I walked over and said in a deep, Russian accent, "I will give you some change, by God I will give you some change." When I came to my senses he was dead and my suit was beyond repair. I felt sick. I called Nick Owen who walked off the 12th green at Sunningdale and incurred a speeding ticket on the M25 in his rush to help me. We buried the body at sea, on high tide at Holy Island. The sight of Nick Owen's head framed against the breaking dawn while he weighted down the body with his golf clubs was one of the most beautiful sights I have ever seen. Afterwards we went for a cooked breakfast and, despite his protestations, I reimbursed Nick for his golf clubs and we went halves on the speeding ticket. It was simply the right thing to do').

work on Monday evening. I go to church on Sundays so no training. You should know that I play very similar to famous play Samuel etc. I play both legs but very perfect with my rite leg. Can we now go to the business side?

Regards

Your DEADEYE

From: Bob Servant
To: Don Woodward
Subject: Great Photos

Deadeye,
Thanks for the photos which are great if a little confusing. Firstly you seem to have undergone quite a transformation between the three photos? Also, did you not say you were eighteen years old? Fuck me, Deadeye, what was your milk round, the entire Sahara? You're the oldest kid since Krankie.

Bob

From: Don Woodward
To: Bob Servant
Subject: RE: Great Photos

Bob,
My hair has changed between photos and that is all. Yes I am older for my age and this works only to your advantage bob as you will be surprised at my strength. Ok bob time to arrange deal. I have quickly worked out flight and everything, luggage and things like this, then insurance and also equipment and say first week of payment in advance. So bob shall we say $12,000 to get my account started and have me come to you?

You need to show you are honest now Bob because sometimes you speak as if you are not,

DEADEYE

From: Bob Servant
To: Don Woodward
Subject: Celebration

Deadeye,

That all makes perfect sense. OK we are very nearly there now. Deadeye, I just need to know one more thing which is how do you celebrate a goal? As our star signing you will be expected not only to score goals but also to celebrate them in a way that will have tongues wagging from Perth to Carnoustie. How will you, Deadeye The Fleet Footed Wonderboy, wag those tongues? Because I want you to wag them so hard, Deadeye, that you start a tsunami.

And please do not accuse me of not being honest, Deadeye. I care about you so deeply that I think I would be unable to lie to you even if I wanted to. I feel like Sir Bobby Charlton has opened a big bottle labeled 'Honesty' and poured every last drop into my mouth.

Your pal in the bootroom,

Bob

From: Don Woodward
To: Bob Servant
Subject: My celebrations for you

Bob,

This is the last question i will answer to you bob because it is too long now. if you to sign me be fast and also bob this is not right a player like me who has won legue titles should be here to sell himself like the women in the market sell the crayfish.

Ok last answer. When ever I score a goal my state of mind changed and i will be very exited and may be force to run to any angle of the pitch racing my hands and thanking God who give me the opportunity to score. As a striker the only thing that I know that will make the fans exited is scoring goals, when a player is a goal scorer he makes the fans happy and gain the support of the fans which will encourage him to work harder and score more goals for his team.

Right bob i attach full details for the bank transfer. Send $12000 now and then this will be sealed. You are sometimes talking as if not serious for this bob. Let us finish the business and have me there with you making fans happy.

Don and DEADEYE

From: Bob Servant
To: Don Woodward
Subject: I think we can do better than that

Deadeye,

Thanks for getting back to me and I wouldn't dream of treating you like a crayfish because you don't deserve that. I have to say though that your celebration didn't really grab my imagination. Don't worry though because I have had a wee think and come up with an alternative. OK here we go:

GOAL CELEBRATION FOR DEADEYE THE FLEET FOOTED WONDERBOY

For a couple of seconds after the goal just stand there as if you can't believe what's happened, then explode into life.

Run as fast as you can to the away fans and cup your ear as if to say 'You were saying?' Then go down on one knee and pretend to bowl a bowling ball. Stand up and run to the home fans. Point at your smile as if to say 'this is me happy get used to it' then pretend to throw a javelin.

Run as fast as you can to the St John's Ambulance mob. Stand in front of them and pretend to have a heart attack then jump back to your feet and laugh as if to say 'Don't be ridiculous: I'm Deadeye and I'm as fit as a fiddle'.

Run as fast as you can over to a ballboy and ruffle his hair until he laughs then gradually increase how hard you are ruffling his hair until he is on the verge of tears then stop ruffling his hair, pick him up and scream in his ear 'You are the naughtiest boy in Britain'.

Run as fast as you can to the fire exit in the corner of the pitch and out to the street.

Run as fast as you can down Tannadice Street, take a right on Arklay Street and stop at the bus stop on the corner of Dens Road. The bus you want is the number 75 to Broughty Ferry. If you need change for the bus you can get it from Inky Instrell's newsagent next to the bus stop. Take a window seat on the right-hand side of the bus so you get a nice view of the river.

Get off the bus at Broughty Ferry train station and run as fast as you can to Harbour View Road. My house is the one with the Space Age extension. Let yourself in. I'll be asleep in the big armchair with Zulu on the telly with the sound down. Kneel down and wake me up by slowly circling my temples with your fingers. It's possible I'll say something like 'not so firm, Frank'. If so ignore that and don't read anything into it.

When I wake up, look at me with that wonky little smile of yours and say, 'I did it boss. I popped one in the onion bag'.

We'll just ad lib it from there. One thing though, Deadeye, please don't take off your shirt off at any point or you'd be in danger of receiving a yellow card.

NO REPLY

17

The Bob Servant Experience

From: Dr Larry Moore
To: Bob Servant
Subject: Your Transfer Is Ready

Dear Sir,
We have the transfer of money to your account ready right now. Please for the legitimacy of this project I would like you to contact this lawyer with the below information so that he will tell you what is needed to do to enable the transfer of this money take effect legally without any question.

NAME: ADV DAVID MAHLANGU
PHONE: ▪▪▪▪▪▪▪▪▪▪▪
advocatedavidmahlangu@▪▪▪▪▪▪▪▪

Please contact him for we had already told him about you. Ask any question as you contact him and tell him what he will do for you as a good lawyer to enable you receive this fund.

God bless you,
Dr Larry Moore

From: Bob Servant
To: David Mahlangu
Subject: All Very Mysterious

Hello,
I was contacted out of the blue by 'Dr' Larry Moore and asked to get in touch with you. While it is exciting to be given instructions in this way (I feel like I'm in a film or working for MFI[56]) I am afraid I have bigger fish on my plate. However one thing I do need is a lawyer. I used to be represented in my scrapes by Joan Downie up near Dawson Park but she's retired now.

---

56 MI5 possibly? Who knows? I'm afraid I couldn't bring myself to ask Bob about this one, fearing it would lead to some sort of metaphor about cupboards.

Can you 'Rumpole me up'?

Your Servant,

Bob Servant

From: David Mahlangu
To: Bob Servant
Subject: Legal Advice

Bob

Yes i am very top lawyer and I did not expect your mail. I work a lot with international transfers of money if this is it and you are expecting transfer then simply send bank details and the money will be with you very soon. My legal chamber will consult the needful office for such transfer and other different Governmental Parasitical responsible for such Fund to be Transfer as you may advice and get back to you as soon as you fill our two legal forms to stand for you as your legal lawyers here in South Africa.

Once again we thank you for your humble contact to our legal office and promised to out in our legal best to get the total fund in your position as soon as we hear from you. I hereby forward the two Attached Legal Form for you to fill and return to us to enable us proceed accordingly.

Yours Faithfully,

ADV DAVID MAHLANGU (Esq.) Member
MAHLANGU ATTORNEYS
ATTORNEYS AT LAW & SOLICITORS
NO. 157 ALEXANDER DBB C, 133 PRESIDENT STREET
JOHANNESBURG, SOUTH AFRICA
TEL: ███████████
Fax: ███████████

Motto: Your satisfaction is our priority

From: Bob Servant
To: David Mahlangu
Subject: My Apologies

David,
Sorry my mistake, I thought you were based here in Blighty. I need a lawyer and I was interested in handing you the golden lollipop[57] but with

---

[57] I did, however, ask Bob for clarification on this phrase, he said it is 'street slang'. I hope that helps.

you based in South Africa I can't see how that would work, what with the language barrier and the time difference.

Oh well, that's life eh? Life's like a box of spanners, David. You choose a spanner and you stand there and say 'Oh look at me with my spanner'. Hang on. Sorry I think I meant hammers not spanners. Christ, what is it? Look, David, what I'm saying is this, 'put down your spanner and have a good time'.

Your man in the toolbox,

Bob

From: David Mahlangu
To: Bob Servant
Subject: This is no problem

Sir

We received your mail and all you said is well noted. In fact these are not any concerns. We have full international clearance to act in Great Britain and also we speak perfect English as you can see. As for time difference well Bob there is just one hour in difference so again do not worry about this.

However Sir, it is our humble respect to inform you that this is our 16 years in the office for this reason we are not ready to stand for any case or project that will bring our legal name down. For this reason we requested that you should fill our legal forms as stated and send it back to us and expect our legal advice by tomorrow after our legal findings as we promised in our first mail.

This is true what you say about life you should not expect the expected ever.

Thank you with peace,

Yours Faithfully,

ADV DAVID MAHLANGU (Esq.) Member

From: Bob Servant
To: David Mahlangu
Subject: You've got the gig

David,
OK that's great news. Well in that case I am very pleased to announce that you, David Mahlangu, are now my lawyer. My man in the trenches if you like, to cover my charge and chuck a couple of grenades at the boo boys.

I have to say what you told me about South Africa made me feel like Bruno Brookes was pushing my brain through a sieve. I didn't know you lot spoke the Queen's lingo and I'm absolutely knocked for six by the one hour situation.

How about a wee side deal, David? If you're an hour ahead then why don't you send me through horse racing results and I could nip down to the bookies and clean up. We could be majorly Geldoffed up here David or, as you say, 'totally Mandela'd'.

Are you ready to hear about the case? It's about being the public eye and what it can do to you. Think of Kinnock headbutting his wife on the beach, double it and add 32.[58]

Bob

From: David Mahlangu
To: Bob Servant
Subject: Tell me everything

Sir

We thank you once more for your fast reply believing that we will not let you down in any way. The one difference is not this simple Bob. In fact we are both existing at the same point in time it is just the clocks that are different. But do not worry about this, it is not vital.

You must tell me about your case Bob as I am your lawyer. Leave nothing out. And I would ask you to provide proof that you will be in a position to pay for our serviced by sending quickly your main banking information.

You need not to worry about my legal chamber representing you as your legal attorney for this transfer, all we are trying to do is to be a good lawyer to you. Note once more that we don't work blindly in any case or any transaction or project for our legal protection and respect. We pray that you give us this trust.

---

58 I imagine Bob is referring to an incident at the 1983 Labour Party conference in Blackpool. Neil Kinnock, the firebrand Labour leader, was walking along the town's beach in full view of the press pack when he lost his footing on the pebbles. Kinnock fell backwards and, in his romantic reluctance to let go of his wife's hand, took her down also. After a few seconds of clumsy squirming, the Kinnocks managed to clamber to their feet and energetically laugh off the mishap. Many commentators have suggested the incident helped lose Kinnock the following General Election, confirming the old adage that no-one wants a Prime Minister who can't walk along a beach without falling over and dragging his wife down with him. Needless to say, Bob's memory of Kinnock headbutting his wife at any stage of proceedings is entirely false.

Thank you with peace,

Yours Faithfully,

ADV DAVID MAHLANGU (Esq.)

From: Bob Servant
To: David Mahlangu
Subject: I'm on the case (no pun intended)

David,

OK I am going to sit down this evening with a flask of OVD and write out the whole sorry story. In a nutshell it's a bust-up with my neighbour Frank that makes Pearl Harbor look like Alton Towers.

Oh and don't worry about me paying you. In the 1980s I made more money than Anna Ford. I was a windowcleaning supremo then a cheese burger van messiah and if you add those two together, David, then the answer is my house which is known round here as Bob's Palace. I attach a photo.

How is your day going? Are you sitting working away with your white wig on?

Yours,

Bob

59

---

59 This isn't Bob's house. In fact, it's the imposing Edinburgh retreat of the much-imitated Scottish writer Irvine 'Big Irv' Welsh. *This photo copyright © Scottish Celebrity Homes Magazine Ltd.*

From: David Mahlangu
To: Bob Servant
Subject: I am ready

Good evening Bob,
I hope you are advance in your notes because I am ready to here the case now Bob. You have a very interesting house and I am sure that you have been a big success in business and in fact I will do a special deal for you because of our mutual standing. So let me hear the case for now and then we can firm a fee Bob.

We only wear wigs when we are in court. Today I am in business suit in office Bob as I have a string of vital meetings.

Your lawyer,

ADV DAVID MAHLANGU (Esq.)

From: Bob Servant
To: David Mahlangu
Subject: Here you are

David,
I hope the string of meetings went well. Sometimes I wish I had become something important and influential like a lawyer or a PE teacher. I certainly never had a string of meetings when I worked on the cheeseburger vans. I was lucky if I had a string of string. Anyway, let's not get bogged down in the string stuff because we could go back and forth on that all night.

Here's the whole sorbet[60] story. As you will have gathered by the way I conduct myself, I am an enormous success story. I have made a lot of money in business and because of my outgoing personality and stuff with my eyes I have built up a large following of fans and imitators.

I don't know what it's like over in South Africa but in Blighty in the last few years there has been all this celebrity stuff. I just don't get it. These days people just seem to be famous for the sake of being famous, like the folk on reality TV and Cliff Thorburn.

Dundee hasn't got that many famous faces so I have been pushed into the limelight. People are coming from all over the place to see me and my big house. I play deaf when they ring the bell and they can't get in because my house is like Fort Nob[61] but Frank's garden next door offers a pretty good view of my place.

---

60 Sordid? Morbid?
61 Fort Knox, presumably. I'd like to think that Bob isn't childish enough for this to be a deliberate error.

In the last few weeks Frank has started allowing people to pay £5 to stand in his garden and watch me. He calls it 'The Bob Servant Experience' and, as you'd expect, it's been very popular. Every time I go out my door there's someone watching and they can see in some of my windows as well. I feel like the whole world is gaping at me and passing judgement. It's like being on trial at Nuremberg, or being Cliff Thorburn.

You've got to help me, David, how can I stop this? I just went out to get a paper and I attach a photo of what was waiting for me. The man shouted that he was 'an admirer' and I shouted back that he was an animal.

Help.

From: David Mahlangu
To: Bob Servant
Subject: I can handle this for you

Hello Bob,

Well Bob this is not a normal situation in any way but we are a legal team who can think fast bob and so we can react to this in the proper way. Your friend does not have the right to do this bob that is very clear to me but it is not as simple as that. It must be proved in court that he is casuing you distress and behaving in a way against the law. This is where I help you Bob using all my experience to make these points to the court in a clear manner because this cannot be done by any man on the street of course.

Ok bob i hope you can see that we are on the right track to ending the behaviour of frank. I will also push for full refund from frank to you of all the money these people have paid because he is getting rich bob from your efforts and your famous nature in the neighbourhood.

Your lawyer,

ADV DAVID MAHLANGU (Esq.)

From: Bob Servant
To: David Mahlangu
Subject: They're in the garden

David,

Thanks for your advice. You certainly sound like you know your business and I like the sound of getting the entrance money off Frank. I looked after that guy for forty years through my various businesses and now he's throwing egg all over my face and legs.

Things have stepped up a notch here tonight. I'd finished my dinner and went out to the garden to have a wee think about what bits of my dinner I'd liked the best when I nearly jumped out of my skin because there was some boy in the bushes. I didn't see him at first then he whispered 'I love everything about you'. I managed to get a photo before running back inside while he shouted after me 'keep doing what you're doing!'

That's me back in the house now, David, and I'm shaking like a horse. Frank's obviously started letting people over his wall and the situation is just completely out of hand. I feel under physical threat in my own home. Like the youngest Walton or Richard Madeley. It's getting towards the winter here, David, I can't risk getting trapped in the house.

I really appreciate your help here, David, in what must have be the toughest case you've ever faced. You must feel like Karl Kennedy[62] during the Cuban Missile Crisis.

Bob

---

62 I presume Bob refers to the late American President John F. Kennedy. Karl Kennedy is a fictional character in the Australian soap opera *Neighbours* and therefore had no impact over, or indeed reaction to, the 1962 Cuban Missile Crisis. Karl Kennedy has suffered great woes during nearly two decades on *Neighbours*, none more so than when his wife Susan (played with great composure by Jackie Woodburne) suffered the extremely rare affliction of retrograde amnesia and forgot her entire past. As can easily be imagined, this caused great strain on the Kennedys' marriage, which had already been tested to the limit by Karl's two extra-marital affairs: first his kissing of receptionist Sarah Beaumont and then his indulging in a torrid affair with *femme fatale* Isabelle 'Issy' Hoyland. Recently, the Kennedys have been placed under further trauma when their adopted son Zeke also suffered retrograde amnesia. The chances of two family members suffering retrograde amnesia are so infinitesimal that the family, understandably, reacted with absolute dismay.

From: David Mahlangu
To: Bob Servant
Subject: The way forward

OK Bob,
You are right it is time to act because no one should be on your property
that is a whole new level. No matter how much people want to see you
and talk to you this is clear illegal and will be easy for me to prove and
put a stop to.

Bob send me $2500 through the Western Union details i gave. I will
then file an EMERGENCY ORDER through all international criminal
courts. This will give police in every country full power to arrest
FRANK and throw him in the jail with the theifs for what he is doing to
do.

You are right bob you should not take more of this and just send the
money and it will be stopped.

Your lawyer,

ADV DAVID MAHLANGU (Esq.)

From: Bob Servant
To: David Mahlangu
Subject: There's hundreds of them

David,
Thanks for your kind words which have been the silver lining to a very
tough day because things are going from bad to worse. Frank has started
bringing in coach tours from Perth. Perth's not the most exciting place in

the world[63] so apparently through there they see me as a mix between David Niven and bubbly former Home Secretary Kenneth Clarke.

   I just tried to nip out the house to go for a pint at Stewpot's and was greeted by the sight below. I tried to get through them but they were like a pack of alligators. They were pulling at my clothes and saying things like

'What's your favourite colour?'

And

'You've changed my life'.

And

'Stop ignoring your fans'.

In the end I had to run back into the house. This is a nightmare, David, and you're the only man who can wake me up. It's like I'm tossing and turning in my bed and you're standing holding a bucket of special lawyer water. Douse me, David. Douse me.

Bob

From: David Mahlangu
To: Bob Servant
Subject: Go to Western Union by the back

Yes Bob I know it is a nightmare that is why I have told you very clearly the instruction to send me $2500. Do this today bob you can get out to a Western Union just for this i am sure even if you must leave by the back of the house.

---

63 See *The Perth Advertiser*, 18 May 2011: *'Opening Hours Extension Rejected'*. ('Perth Town Council today rejected a motion that would have extended public house opening hours to 10 p.m. "This is not the Wild West," said a council spokesman, "or some sort of rock and roll anything goes fiesta party place." ').

These people are all breaking the law and i will treat them like the dogs they are in the courtroom bob this is my grave promise to you bob but first you must send the money for me to file the EMERGENCY ORDER.

This is vital go now bob go out of the back of the house to a Western UNION

ADV DAVID MAHLANGU (Esq.)

From: Bob Servant
To: David Mahlangu
Subject: Surrounded

David,

I'm afraid that won't work because I'm completely surrounded. I was up first thing this morning and darted out the front door to try and get to the bank and sort your fee when I was greeted with this –

I don't think I've ever seen that many people David, not all at once anyway. They went absolutely potty when they saw me and started chanting. The chant went like this –

We want Bob
We want Bob
Two pork chops and a corn on the cob
We want Bob
We want Bob
Harrison Ford has lost his job

Any idea what they're singing about, David? Where does Harrison Ford come into it? If he's lost his job then it's the first I've heard of it. It's not like

he's done a Dave Lee Travis. Remember that one, David? When Dave Lee
Travis resigned live on air and sawed off his own leg?[64]

Anyway I was pretty shaken up by how many people were out there,
and a bit thrown by the whole Harrison Ford thing, so I went through to my
back bathroom for a bath. When I got out I reached down to pick up my
slippers and I heard all these screams. I turned round and took a quick
snap –

My back was to the window so they must have seen the whole chemistry
set when I bent over. I can't help feeling like I won this round but it's a
hollow victory really, David, like the way Philip Schofield gets called the
'thinking man's crumpet' and keeps winning these prizes meant for skirt.[65]

We need to end this once and for all, David. How?

Bob

From: David Mahlangu
To: Bob Servant
Subject: Is it real?

Bob,
In fact this is just not seeming true now bob. All these people in your
garden? That is a crowd from a sport game bob in the photo you have sent
and that second one is not a real photo you think i will believe this?

---

64 In 1993 the BBC Radio DJ Dave Lee Travis resigned during a live broadcast
in protest at the creative direction of Radio 1. He did not saw off his leg in the
process and remains fully limbed at the time of writing (August 2011).
65 See *The Dundee Evening Telegraph*, 29 August 2010: ' "Humbled" Schofield
wins Rear of The Year again'.

Send the money now if you want me to respresent you and explain your position again because now it is different to what i thought and it is not seeming true to me. You must tell me different now bob your bill is already high so every way means you should send the $2500.

ADV DAVID MAHLANGU (Esq.)

From: Bob Servant
To: David Mahlangu
Subject: The Final Insult

David,

Bit of a weird one. Frank came round and we had a chat. We talked about all the good times we've had. I pointed out everything I've done for him over the years and how I took him under my belt and showed him a life that he could never even have imagined. He said it sounded like Pretty Woman and I said that's fine for him to say that it was like Pretty Woman as long as he is very clear on the fact that it is like Pretty Woman without the sauce and he said that went without saying and I said actually I'd rather it didn't go without saying particularly if anyone else is around when he says it. He said that he was sorry and that I was still his boss after all and he should have treated me with more respect and I said he was also jealous of my success and he said well that's probably something we should put to one side and I said in fact it was probably more appropriate if we talked about it at length and he went a bit red and his eyes started twitching like they did that time before he ▇▇▇▇▇▇ that ▇▇▇▇▇ after that parrot said that his ▇▇▇ looked like a ▇▇▇▇▇▇▇▇▇[66]

Frank headed home so I settled down to a Meat Attack but then ten minutes later the doorbell went and there he was again. He said he wanted to show just how sorry he was and handed me a present of a large tub of margarine. I thanked him and said that if he wanted to go away and come back with a better present that would fine. He smiled and said 'oh I think that will keep you busy for now'. I thought he was having one of his turns so told him to go to bed and went through to my kitchen.

The margarine tub felt quite heavy and I thought I could hear voices but that oftens happens when I've had a Meat Attack so I ignored it and decided to make myself a wee butty. I got out the rolls and opened the tub of margarine and, oh dear God, David. I attach a photo of what was in there. I near enough shat myself. Who wouldn't?

Bob

---

66 Removed on legal advice. See *The Dundee Courier*, 14 May 1983: *'Pet Shop Burnt To The Ground'*.

From: David Mahlangu
To: Bob Servant
Subject: No more

Are you saying to me serious that these people were inside a box of
margarine? Do you think you talk to a child? I hope you can provide a
proper reason for this or you are in bigger trouble than you would know.

18
Why Me? 3

From: Bob Servant
To: Rose
Subject: 'Why Me?'

Rose,
Hope all's well at your end. I've spoken to you a couple of times before about my book. Well, Rose, we've reached the end. The old horse has had one last run round the paddock and now we're all on the bus to the glue factory. What I'm saying to you, Rose, is that the publishers are on my back like monkeys and the printer is sitting with his finger on the big button. I'm under the most awful pressure, Rose. I feel like Agatha Christie at a pub quiz.

I'd love to put our emails in the book, Rose. I think they'd really bring something to the party and also I'd like to use your light-hearted 'Why Me?' gag as the title. What do you think? Come on, Rose, get involved. You owe it to yourself.

Bob

From: Rose
To: Bob Servant
Subject: RE: 'Why Me?'

NO

From: Bob Servant
To: Rose
Subject: re: 'Why Me?'

Rose,
That's fine. I have too much respect for you to ask again.

Your Servant,

Bob Servant

NO REPLY

Acknowledgements

Thanks to – Hugh Andrew, Andrew Simmons and all at Birlinn, David Riding and all at MBA and Michael Munro for their roles in this book. A big 'Dundee hello' to Mum, Dad, Alan and Carol. And greetings, with just the right amount of respect, to my pals from Dundee and beyond. Have a drink on me.[67] Finally, thanks from myself and Bob to the brave, honest people of Broughty Ferry (may your heads remain high). And now, I suppose, to Bob.

I found him sitting in Broughty Ferry's celebrated Stewpot's bar, engrossed in the letters page of the *Dundee Evening Telegraph*. Bob placed the newspaper down, tapped his finger on the letters page and said with a wink that it was 'a good argument for laboratories'. Over the following, uncomfortable half an hour, which included an emotional ten minute conversation where I coaxed Bob back out of a toilet cubicle, it emerged that he had intended to say 'lobotomies'.

From this unpromising start the conversation mended itself by me allowing Bob full reign. He opined at length on the government cutbacks which he seemed to believe had directly caused television advertising breaks to 'double' in length. 'If that's not irony what is?' he asked while I desperately searched for an answer that wouldn't have me back talking to a toilet door.

Bob reserved vitriol for the phone hacking scandal, calling the offending journalists alternatively 'maggots' and 'magpies'. He confessed that he had a personal sense of outrage having been 'targeted' by the *Dundee Courier*. His evidence was shaky at best – he had 'heard someone on his roof a couple of times' and 'a strange Volvo' had started to park on his road. Slightly more sinister was his story of hearing heavy breathing during a recent phone call, though I tactfully identified that Bob had been cutting his grass at the time and had been forced to run for the phone 'like Alan Wells'.[68]

Bob suggested a walk. He led me to Broughty Ferry's harbour where I brought up the Acknowledgements section in which you currently wallow.

---

67 Get a receipt, single house spirits and basic lager only. One per applicant.
68 Wells, Alan (1952–). Popular Scottish sprinter who defied the odds to win gold at the 1980 Moscow Olympic Games. See *The Dundee Courier*, 26 July 1980: '*Brave Scot Ends Communism*'.

Bob was mercilessly swift in providing the sole individual he wanted to thank in print.

'Andre Agassi,' shrugged Bob, 'for showing me that it could be done.' He delivered the line with enough certainty to silence my many questions.

The harbour at Broughty Ferry offers a sweeping view of the surroundings and I asked Bob about his unbreakable attachment with the area.

'This used to be my playground,' he said simply.

It was a whimsical, near poetic touch from Bob that I enjoyed until noticing that Bob was pointing at a children's playground over the road. I asked if he had ever considered leaving the area.

'When you have a nice hat,' said Bob, 'you only take it off to sleep.'

This was followed by an epic tale of a promotion in the *Dundee Courier* in the late 1980s. Bob gravely recalled collecting thirteen daily tokens in a row for a coach trip to the Lake District. Tragically, on the 14th and final day of the promotion Bob did not buy a copy of the newspaper ('Frank's fault, let's leave it at that') and therefore missed out on the coach trip.

'Little twists, eh?' said Bob in conclusion.

He acted out a twisting action that clumsily mutated into the mimed opening of a wine bottle, followed by the mimed pouring and drinking of a glass of wine. Concerned that Bob was planning to drink the whole virtual bottle, I suggested that I walk him home. When we passed Frank's house Bob coughed a couple of times and said that I 'might as well' add in the Acknowledgements that Frank is 'all right'.

Bob and Frank, I should reiterate, have known each other for over fifty years and the erosion that must have caused to Frank's mental health is inconceivable. After only two months in the company of Bob and his emails I had sensed my grip on reality loosening by the day.[69]

Frank was, I suggested, Bob's most trusted friend.

'If he was a dog he'd have been put down,' answered Bob, 'and there have been lots of times that I'd have driven him to the vets. But, put it this way, I wouldn't have watched them do it and I wouldn't have bought another dog.'

I observed that Frank's great strength is surely his loyalty and Bob nodded in agreement.

'He's my Ginger Roger,' he said.

---

69 On that note may I take this late opportunity to clarify that, as far as I am aware, Sir Trevor McDonald has never committed murder. Furthermore, former BBC newsreaders Nicholas Witchell and Moira Stewart have never assisted McDonald in the disposal of a corpse. However, with regard to the suggestion that former *Crimewatch* presenter Nick Owen buried the body of a homeless man at sea please refer to page 164 of *Don't Have Nightmares, Do Sleep Well – The Nick Owen Story* (Foreword by Sir Trevor McDonald).

'Ginger Rogers,' I corrected.

'No, Ginger Roger,' confirmed Bob, before clarifying that he referred to a red-haired man from Lochee who is locally accepted in Dundee as being especially loyal.

We arrived at the gate to Bob's personable house. A building bought and crudely extended with the proceeds of thousands, if not millions, of cheeseburgers. I asked, with some trepidation, of Bob's future plans, aware that I seem to be inextricably part of whatever they may be. I hinted at his thinning years and he replied with a fable involving a jam jar. There was something about the amount of jam being left in a jar, coupled with the quality of the jam and then, most cryptically of all, the tightness of the jar's lid.

'Let me tell you something,' said Bob. 'Dean Martin used to sleep with a ham sandwich beside his bed made out of the best ham in town. He never ate it because he didn't like ham. Someone asked him once why he slept next to a ham sandwich when he didn't like ham and you know what he said? He said, "Because I can." Do you see,' asked Bob, 'what I mean?'

'Yes,' I lied.

Bob shook my hand and walked grandly up his path. He paused, spun round and shouted, 'Which one was "Blue Eyes", "Old Blue Eyes"?'

'Frank Sinatra,' I called back.

'That's who I meant,' Bob shouted urgently. 'It was Frank Sinatra with the ham sandwich. Change it to that and stick it in the book.'

So that's it, my last note as editor. It was Frank Sinatra with the ham sandwich.

NF

Delete This at Your Peril
The Bob Servant Emails

Neil Forsyth

Anti-hero of spam Bob Servant takers on internet fraudsters at their own game in this hilarious compendium of genuine email exchanges. As they entice him with lost African millions, Russian brides and get-rich-quick scams, Bob responds by generously offering some outlandish schemes of his own. The spammers may have breached his firewall, but they have met their match as the former window cleaner and cheeseburger magnate rises heroically to the challenge and sows confusion in his wake.

'A very, very funny book'
Irvine Welsh

'A living, breathing creation of comic genius'
Bookbag

'Genius! Highly entertaining and brilliantly deranged'
Maxim

'Reminds me how good comic writing can be'
Scotland on Sunday

978 1 84158 919 0   £6.99

Bob Servant – Hero of Dundee

Neil Forsyth

Cyber hero Bob Servant became a cult classic in the bestselling *Delete This at Your Peril*. This much-anticipated sequel tells the life story of one of Scotland's unsung heroes. From his days in the Merchant Navy, to his creation of a record-breaking window-cleaning round and his time as a cheeseburger magnate, Bob Servant has lived life to its fullest. With touching bravery he takes the reader on a fearless romp through the hilarious, whimsical and impassioned memories that surely make him the undisputed Hero of Dundee.

'Hilarious. Full of sly Scottish humour'
Martin Kelner

'There's stuff here that Chic Murray would have been proud of'
Sanjeev Kohli

'Crackingly funny . . . There's a laugh on every page'
The Herald

978 1 84158 920 6   £6.99